ESSAYS FOR THE
CHURCH

ESSAYS FOR THE
CHURCH

Foundational Christian Theology
for a Stronger Faith

JOE DERQUE
EDITED BY BEAU C. DERQUE

XULON ELITE

Xulon Press Elite
2301 Lucien Way #415
Maitland, FL 32751
407.339.4217
www.xulonpress.com

Paperback ISBN-13: 978-1-6628-4792-9
Ebook ISBN-13: 978-1-6628-4793-6

FOREWORD

This is a book on systematic theology, which is the discipline of interpreting the Bible literally, as it was intended, and by understanding its passages in the manner they were intended by their authors and in the way they were understood by their original readers. Proper systematic theology seeks to place the Scriptures in their accurate historical context and in the context of the passage itself, the book it was written in, and the Bible as a whole. The point is to achieve theological consistency throughout the entire Bible. The systematic method contained in this book is one deriving from the Evangelical, Dispensational viewpoint.

The book contains essays on many of the foundational beliefs of the Christian faith. I believe that we, as Christians, are in desperate need of a clear understanding of the basis of our faith and what the Bible actually says. In many Christian churches today we have wandered doctrinally well away from the actual teachings of the Bible.

This book is intended to strengthen our faith, our resolve, and our courage in very difficult times, which are likely to become even more challenging in the future. It is also my hope that I have managed to answer many of the truly difficult questions that are asked by current Christians, searchers, and the lost.

ACKNOWLEDGMENTS

To my wife of almost 50 years, Nancy, who married me when I was lost and, in her own way, led me on the road to salvation. Next, to Pastor Mike Goodwin, now retired from Faith Baptist Church in Festus/Crystal City, MO, who taught me the systematic, dispensational theology that I still follow today. Also, to my younger son, Beau, who was my faithful computer tool driver and editor and without whom this book would not have happened. And to my friends, Mike and Dianna Bond, and my brother-in-law Grant Vaughn, for their years of encouragement and faith in me, particularly when I became totally discouraged. Finally, to Jesus, the Risen Christ, who carried me and my family through the tough times.

Joe Derque, Jefferson City, MO, 3/20/2022

If you have questions or comments, we encourage you to contact Joe by E-Mail at:
essaysforthechurch@yahoo.com

TABLE OF CONTENTS

Chapter 1:
ON GOD

(The Book of Jonah)
"He's a walkin' contradiction...takin' every wrong
direction on his lonely way back home."
- Kris Kristofferson, *Pilgrim 33*

INTRODUCTION AND BACKGROUND

The Prophet Jonah is noted as being one of the oldest recorded Prophets in the Old Testament. Only Obadiah and Joel are known to have preceded Jonah.[1] Jonah was God's Prophet (or one of them) to the Northern Kingdom of Israel under Jeroboam II (794 BC–753 BC).[2] Second Kings 14:25 recorded some military expansion, actually reconquest by Jeroboam, of land in Northern Palestine that reached up to the Northern boundary of the original Promised Land. This land was retaken from the Assyrians "In accordance with the word of the Lord ...spoken through his servant Jonah" (2 Kings 14:25). Jonah may have also been a contemporary of both Hosea and

---

[1] Charles Caldwell Ryrie, *The Ryrie Sturdy Bible, Expanded Edition, NIV* (Chicago: Moody Press, 1994) 1017

[2] Ibid., 1369

Amos.[3] Jonah was, up to the point of the occurrence in the Book of Jonah, a successful good news prophet.

Regarding the author, much has been made of the otherworldly nature of the book of Jonah and the accompanying supernatural events in it. These events include Jonah spending time inside a big fish, the unlikely repentance of the Ninevites, the appearance and disappearance of the castor plant, and the scorching wind brought about solely for Jonah's benefit. In addition, the book is written as a narrative in the third person and partly in past tense. Also, some criticism has been leveled at the large size of Nineveh as portrayed in the book. Critics conclude that the book was written as a post-exilic allegory rather than an accurate, historical account written by Jonah.[4]

It must first be pointed out that some critical scholars embrace materialism and rationalism, called by John Hannah "antisupernaturalism,"[5] and therefore disregard anything in the Bible that cannot be scientifically or rationally explained and isn't confined to known activities in the physical world. Beginning with that assumption in mind, of course, most of the Bible would be regarded as a complete fairy tale.

Support of the accuracy of the book, however, begins with the fact that Jesus regarded Jonah as historical in Matthew 12:40–41 and in the parallel verse in Luke 11:30–32. To say that Jesus, God on Earth in human form, didn't know His own Scriptures would be ludicrous. Further, Jonah used real names

---

[3] Ibid., 1017

[4] John D. Hannah, *The Bible Knowledge Commentary,* John F. Walvoord and Roy B. Zuck, Editors (Colorado Springs: David C. Cook, 1984) 1462

[5] Ibid., 1462-1463

and real places[6] that seem to coincide with real historic events involving Nineveh and the Assyrians[7]. Examples would be the known disasters that befell Nineveh, likely prior to Jonah's visit, including a famine in 765 BC, a total solar eclipse in 763 BC, and another famine in 759 BC, thus preparing Nineveh for Jonah's message.[8] Additionally, Jonah is identified at the beginning of the book as a real person, and placed in a historic time and place in 2 Kings 14:25, unlike an allegorical tale i.e. "Once upon a time in a land far, far away." Finally, Jonah did not appear in the book as a heroic figure, but was characterized as a prophet with a bad attitude. Since it is unlikely that a Jew of a later time would make up such an unflattering story about a Jewish prophet, it is likely that Jonah wrote the book himself, probably as part of his vow (Jonah 2:9).

We also must take a brief look at the Assyrians. Nineveh, and two or three surrounding communities, are regarded as being an ancient metropolitan area of some size, and the capital of the Assyrian Empire.[9] The King of Nineveh (Jonah 3:6) was likely the king of the whole Assyrian Empire, probably Ashur-dan III (772–754 BC).[10] Jonah stated (Jonah 3:3), that a visit to Nineveh required three days (NIV). Charles Caldwell Ryrie believed that to be the time it took to walk around the circumference of the whole metropolitan area. Jonah also recorded a population of at least 120,000 (Jonah 1:10), which was quite large for an Ancient Near East (ANE) city.

---

[6] Mark Deaver, *The Message of the Old Testament* (Wheaton: Crossway Books, 2006) 770

[7] Hannah, Ibid., 1462 et seq.

[8] Ibid.

[9] Hannah, Ibid., 1463

[10] Ryrie, Ibid., 1369

The Assyrians were, at the time and up until their conquest by the Babylonian Empire in 612 BC,[11] the most feared of Israel's neighbors. Elliot Johnson said, "Nineveh was the capital of one of the cruelest, vilest, most powerful, and most idolatrous empires in the world."[12] The Assyrians eventually overcame the Northern Kingdom, in 722 BC, and took them into exile, from which the ten tribes of the Northern Kingdom never returned. Warfare in the ANE, among the mostly pagan nations, was a shockingly brutal affair. The pagan nations, up to and including the ancient Greeks, had no scruples, standards, conventions of warfare, or moral barriers to restrain them. There were no rules and no prohibitions. Regarded at the time as the worst of the bunch were the Persians, followed closely by the Assyrians. The Babylonians probably deserve an honorable mention here.[13] As Ryrie said, the Persians (and the Assyrians) had a notable disregard and "complete disdain" of human life.[14] Being located on the northeastern border of Israel, the Assyrians were the Jew's worst nightmare.

JONAH CHAPTER 1

The Book of Jonah opens with the identification of Jonah, typical of a legitimate Prophet of God in the Bible. Jonah is also identified in 2 Kings 14:25, which puts Jonah as a prophet during the reign of Jeroboam II of Israel (the Northern Kingdom) from

---

[11] Robert B. Chisholm, Jr., Handbook on the Prophets (Grand Rapids: Baker Academic, 2002) 431

[12] Johnson, Elliott E., The Bible Knowledge Commentary, Ibid. 1493-1494

[13] Ryrie, Ibid., 736

[14] Ibid.

793 BC to 753 BC. Jonah wrote the book of Jonah about 760 BC. Jonah was from Gath Hepher, a town in the Tribe of Zebulon.[15]

A word about true prophets of God is in order here. Jonah is identified as a prophet of God in 2 Kings 14:25 because of a successful prediction he made. It should be noted that it was a positive prediction, that said something good would happen to Israel, and it did. Generally, being a true prophet of God, whom God actually spoke to, was a very tough assignment. One need only read about the careers of Jeremiah or Elijah (1 and 2 Kings) to realize that being God's prophet was, likely as not, going to set the prophet at complete odds with the socio/cultural belief system of the time and with the governing powers of the nation as well. Being a prophet of God was also a dangerous undertaking. Jeremiah was rescued from death by slow starvation and deprivation only by the fall of Jerusalem and a friend (Jer. 37–38). Elijah had to seek God's special protection to return from hiding on Mt. Horeb (1 Kings 19:11–13). Anecdotally, it is thought that Isaiah ended his career because he was murdered by Manasseh, another Jewish king who didn't like bad news. Jonah had been a good news prophet up to that time and likely had an elevated position and some authority in the community as a result.

That would all change because, in the first two verses of Jonah, God gave Jonah a very simple command that Jonah doesn't like at all. God said, "Go to the great city of Nineveh and preach against it, because its wickedness has come up before me" (Chapter 1: 2). As has been said, the Ninevites were both hated and feared by their neighbors. In addition to the usual depravities of pagan worship, the Assyrians were known for their barbaric treatment of prisoners. The last thing Jonah wanted to

---

[15] Hannah, Ibid., 1461

do was go there and be the vehicle for the repentance of the Ninevites. Likely, Jonah wanted a word from God to deliver to the Jews, guaranteeing the impending destruction of the Ninevites instead. Not only was Jonah extremely angry with this assignment, but he also had good reason to be frightened. Knowing the proclivities of the Assyrians, Jonah could not help but believe that, upon delivery of the message from the God of Israel, Jonah, the formerly successful prophet, would find his skin hanging from the walls of Nineveh. Jonah was both angry and frightened because his whole world was about to fall apart, and that was only if he survived the ordeal. Jonah believed he was sent on a suicide mission.

So, in Chapter 1 vs. 3, Jonah did the only sensible thing he could think of. He ran away from God. Going to Joppa, now Jaffa and part of the Tel Aviv port and metropolitan area, Jonah got the first (likely Phoenician) ship out for Tarshish. Nineveh is about five hundred miles East by Northeast from Northern Israel. Tarshish was a Phoenician city about 1,500 miles West of Joppa, in Southern Spain just past Gibraltar. It was as far west as Phoenician sailors would dare go and was considered the west end of the known world.[16] In other words, it was as far away from God as Jonah thought he could get.

This is not quite as silly as it sounds to us. There might be some religious syncretism here between the Jews and some of the pagan beliefs in Jonah's thinking. The various tribes and nations in the ANE, pagan one and all, basically had somewhat the same pagan beliefs and customs but many different names for their own personal gods. All were loosely derivative of the Sumerian goddess Ishtar, who oversaw love and war. Male pagan gods included Bel, Baal, Molech (or Moloch), and

---

[16] Hannah, Ibid., 1465

Dagon. Pagan worship seemed to be much the same between various gods, all involving liquor, illicit sex, and dancing around the infamous Asherah poles together with an occasional child sacrifice. Another commonality was the general belief that gods were local and had decreasing power the farther away from the borders of their area one went. Pagans had to carry their gods of "wood and stone" with them for their gods to have any power in their immediate vicinity. Pagan gods weren't necessarily universal either. They were more regarded as specific gods for specific people. The Old Testament often speaks in terms of "my god and your God." So different gods could have charge of different places and people. Finally, and as it particularly relates to the Jews, a lot of the events of the Old Testament carried an underlying current of being a contest between The God of the Jews and the pagan deities of various other nations as to which deity was more powerful. An early example of that is the contest between Moses and the Egyptian Pharaoh (Exod. 5:1 to 12:36) to free God's people. This can be seen as a direct challenge by God to the supposed power of many of the major pagan gods in the Egyptian pantheon, and in the pagan gods' own territory. In this powerful object lesson, God showed both the Egyptians and the Jews that He was the Living God of all creation, and the only God.

So, Jonah tried running away anyway. He didn't get too far. Chapter 1: 4–11 describes a violent storm that was sent by God, which threatened the ship and everyone on it. It is interesting to note that all the sailors (likely Phoenician idol worshipers) "each cried out to his own god" (Chapter 1: 5), indicating not only regional and national gods, but various household gods as well. All of the pagan gods were apparently out of range because the captain of the ship had to wake Jonah to get him to "call on [his] god, maybe he will take notice" (Chapter 1:6). In the meantime, the sailors cast lots to find out whose god was out to get them. Casting lots is a long-time superstition in the Old Testament that even extends to the New Testament, when the Apostles, rightly or wrongly, cast lots to decide who would replace Judas as the twelfth apostle (Acts 1:23–26). Jonah lost the lottery and the sailors immediately questioned him. They asked him who he was, but the most interesting question was, "Who is responsible for making all this trouble for us?" (Chapter 1:8). What they wanted to know was not what Jonah had done to anger his God, but whose God could possibly be powerful enough to raise an apocalyptic storm like the one they were in. Jonah, somewhat repentant, told them his God created the "sea and the land" (Chapter 1:9).

The sailors then asked what they could do to make God happy again and Jonah told them to throw him in. They did not want to do that, so they tried rowing to shore in an effort to save the ship and everyone in it. In Chapter 1:10-16 when the sea became even worse and they couldn't reach land, the sailors were forced to throw Jonah overboard, but only after praying to God not to be held accountable for the murder. This is an interesting note because at the same time that Jonah was having a crisis of faith, the pagan sailors seemed to embrace God as the real thing, fearing Him and offering vows and a sacrifice (Chapter 1:16).

At the end of chapter one, Jonah was swallowed by a great fish, sent by God. Jonah spent "three days and three nights" (Chapter 1:17) inside the fish. To the Ancient Hebrews, three days required only twenty-four hours plus parts of two other days.[17] This was probably Jesus' "sign of Jonah" (Matthew 12:20), reflecting Christ's own burial and resurrection.

---

[17] Ryrie, Ibid., 1372

JONAH CHAPTER 2

Chapter two breaks from the narrative form and is a prayer by Jonah offered from inside the fish. Most of the prayer is written in the past tense, seemingly recorded by Jonah after he was thrown up on shore. This also supports the proposition that part of Jonah's vow was to write down his story. The other part of the vow was doubtless for Jonah to obey God next time.

Jonah's prayer reflected two things regarding Jonah; that Jonah believed going to hell consisted of a complete separation from God—being profoundly lost and hopeless ("To the roots of the mountains I sank down; the earth beneath barred me in forever.") (Chapter 2:6), and that Jonah, believing that he was going to die, repented of his foolishness and placed his complete faith back in God ("Salvation comes from the Lord" (Chapter 2:9).

As a final thought, Jonah's prayer had all the basic elements of the conditional prayer God gave to Solomon, for the people, in 2 Chronicles 7:14. Jonah appeared to be very humble, having experienced both God's power and anger due to disobedience. Jonah sought God's face as his only recourse. He made a vow to God that he swore to keep as a demonstration of turning from his wicked ways and showing repentance.

The result, in the last verse of Chapter 2, had God hearing Jonah's petition and commanding the great fish to throw Jonah up on dry land.

JONAH CHAPTER 3

Chapter three opens with the word of the Lord coming to Jonah a second time, with the same message as first spoken in Jonah 1:2. We don't know if any time elapsed between Jonah's ordeal with the great fish or if the word of the Lord came to Jonah immediately after he hit the beach. Regardless, Jonah got the message. "Jonah obeyed the word of the lord and went to Nineveh" (Chapter 3:3).

As it has been said, Nineveh was a large metropolitan community. Jonah spent three days walking and preaching through the whole town. The message, simply put, was "repent, or else." Something resembling the Great Awakenings of past centuries in America then took place. In Chapter 3:5 it states, "The Ninevites believed God." The Ninevites repented, fasted, and put on sackcloth and ashes. When word reached the king, he led by example and not only put on sackcloth, but also went out and sat in the dirt in the middle of town. He issued a decree ordering everyone to "give up their evil ways" and, most interestingly, said "Who knows? God may yet relent" (Chapter 3:9).

While the reaction of the Ninevites is extraordinary, and shows the extraordinary power of the Holy Spirit, the profound lesson in this chapter may be the forgiveness and compassion God showed for His creation, including animals (Jonah 4:11). As has been said, the Assyrians were not noted for their kindness toward their enemies and probably not toward each other either. The ANE generally was a cruel and very tough historical period and, as Thomas Hobbes said in *Leviathan*, life was "nasty, brutish, and short." In addition, the "God of the Old Testament" is thought by some to be mean, vindictive, judgmental, and unforgiving. Nothing could be farther from the truth. The Book of Jonah is just one startling example of the mercy, grace, and forgiveness of God, regardless of whether the recipients deserve it or not.

JONAH CHAPTER 4

God's compassion, ironically, angered Jonah greatly (Jonah 4:1).[18] There might be several reasons for Jonah's attitude problem. First, while Jonah preached imminent destruction as God's message to Assyria, after the Ninevites repented, God found the compassion and grace to spare them. As has been said, the Assyrians were blood enemies of the Jews. Some commentators believe Jonah was familiar with the prophecies of Amos and Hosea and knew Assyria would destroy the Northern Kingdom (Hannah, 1470).[19] So Jonah much preferred to see God destroy the Ninevites on the spot. Further, Jonah knew that he would be accused of being a false prophet. He delivered a message of destruction, but God relented and spared Nineveh, as Jonah knew He would (Chapter 4:1-2). In addition, Jonah would be regarded by the Jews as being responsible for the salvation of Israel's worst enemy. Jonah saw his status and career in the Northern Kingdom going from success and fame to exclusion, danger, and persecution, much like Elijah before him and Jeremiah after him.

Jonah's anger at God also reflects the exclusivist and nationalist attitude of the Jews. This exclusivist attitude was not God's original intent, but it persisted and probably grew worse through the First Century AD. In Exodus 12:38 and Exodus 12:48, "other people" left Egypt with the Jews and, if they wanted to adopt God's requirements, they became "like one born in the land." Moses had, perhaps, two wives. Zipporah, his first wife, was a Midianite (Ex. 2:16–21), and a "woman from Cush" was apparently a second wife (Numbers 12:1). Ruth, great-grandmother

---

[18] Ryrie, Ibid., 1373, the word literally means "hot"

[19] Hannah, Ibid., 1470

of King David and therefore in Jesus' lineage, was a Moabite. None of the three women were Jews. Jesus went out of His way to take salvation to the Samaritans, who were mixed race, practiced a syncretistic religion, and were despised by the Jews. He was chided for that by his disciples (John 4:4–42). Finally, the Apostle Paul insisted that God was the Lord of all, and that Jesus brought salvation to everyone, regardless of race or societal status (Romans 10:12). Paul suffered greatly for his theology, being victimized repeatedly by the "Judaizers." The Judaizers were Jews who believed in exclusivism, i.e. that one had to become Jewish to share in the Jew's exclusive God. The Judaizers persecuted Paul on several occasions (Acts 13–15).

In Chapter 4:1–5, a very angry Jonah walked out of the city and up to a hillside where he made a shelter and sat down to see what would happen to the Assyrians. Jonah was so disgusted and depressed by that time that he preferred to die (Chapter 4:3). In the face of all this anger, God responded with a gentle question: "Have you any right to be angry?" (Chapter 4:4). The King James Version states "Doest thou well to be angry?" which may contain a little deeper thought than the New International Version. Not only did Jonah have no right to be angry at God, he also didn't help himself at all by harboring anger and bitterness, particularly toward God. While we can certainly question God, being angry with Him is a negative emotion that we should avoid. Being angry at God shows a lack of maturity, selfishness, lack of humility, and a complete misunderstanding of who God is. It is one thing to have human doubts. It's entirely another to stand in intentional, determined opposition to God, particularly when we think God doesn't act the way we think He ought to.

In the last verses of the book (Chapter 4:5–10) God provided an object lesson for Jonah. First, God sent a large, shady plant to shelter Jonah from the sun and the heat. The next day God not only removed the sheltering plant but also sent a hot, dry wind to add to Jonah's misery (called a *sirocco* in the middle east and a *Santa Ana* in California). Jonah not only remained angry, but also suffered greatly from the heat. Jonah stated, in fact, that he was still "angry enough to die" (Jonah 4:9b). God then delivered His message to Jonah, which ends the book and serves as the lesson of the story.

God pointed out to Jonah that Jonah was more concerned about the plant that gave him comfort and, by extension, his own people and his own career, than the people of Nineveh. God delivered the lesson that the 120,000 people of Nineveh (plus their animals), had as they were, were *all* God's creation, which He loved as much as He loved the Jews, and which God was desirous to redeem.

APPLICATION

The first practical application of the Book of Jonah might be a lesson in putting Christianity into action in our lives. While it might be difficult for us, as it was for Jonah, when God calls us to action we should listen and go. We often hear from the pulpit sermons on the "comfortable Christian," typically contrasted with Isaiah 6:8, "Here am I. Send me!" As frequent as those messages are, the point is not to just go do something. The point is to grow quiet and listen to what God is asking or calling us to do, and then obey. Much is said in the Old Testament, particularly in the Psalms, and in the New Testament by Jesus (Matt. 7:13–14), in regard to one's walk with the Lord, walking the straight path, and taking the narrow road. The straight path, or narrow road, is the direction God wants us to go and the life God wants us to lead. From listening and obedience comes blessed living and a victorious life, a life lived the way God intended for us. Far too often we ignore the "still, small voice" (1 Kings 19:12) and turn from the straight path to embrace the noise, greed, and hubris of the world around us. Jonah displayed a little hubris when he wanted to decide for himself what the fate of the Ninevites should be. We display the same hubris when we decide to ignore what God asks us to do and how God asks us to conduct our lives and embrace the man-made standards of the world.

Second, our God is truly the God of the second chance. The Bible is full of deeply flawed humans who received grace, redemption, forgiveness, and a second chance from a very gracious God. It has been said that one of the major overall themes of the Bible, both Old Testament and New Testament, is God's grace toward His creation. Abram and Sarai both laughed in disbelief at God but got a second chance. Moses repeatedly argued with God, but God always gave both Moses—and particularly the Israelites—a second chance. King David was shocking in his adulterous and murderous behavior, but repented, sought forgiveness, and received a second chance. The apostle Paul was the second chance champion of the New Testament, having actually helped stone to death Stephen, a faithful Christian. Next, of course, was the apostle Peter who, in spite of having strayed from the path several times, including multiple denials of Jesus, received a second chance from the Risen Lord. And finally, Jonah, sitting on the beach, having just been, almost literally, resurrected from the dead, got a second chance to be the prophet God wanted him to be.

It is important to note that Jesus took His ministry to the truly lost and broken in the society of His day, and received the best response from that group. Those folks included the poor, the disenfranchised, tax collectors, Samaritans, the unclean, the physically stricken, Roman pagans, and women of ill repute. All of them got a second chance. So, when we deliver the message, particularly to the lost, hurt, and broken of our society, we need to remember Jonah and introduce people to the God of the second chance.

Finally, and particularly striking to me, was God's quiet question to Jonah, "Do you well to be angry?" (Jonah 4:4, KJV). What we see so much today, even in the pastorate in some churches and in some of our seminaries, are people who, at some point, became angry at God, and decide to replace the God of the Bible with one they create themselves. Even though God provided multiple miracles for Jonah and for Nineveh, Jonah was angry with God because God didn't act the way Jonah wanted Him to. At the end of the book, Jonah was still pouting. How often do we do that? How often do we blame things on God that are the fault of our own sin and the result of living in a lost and dying world? How often do we place the blame for failure on a capricious God rather than on ourselves and our own faults and ineptitude? How often do we ignore and discount Satan and our own miserable behavior as being the cause of our problems, and become angry at God? We become angry at God because He doesn't see things our way or do what we want Him to do. Then we create a god of "wood and stone" that always agrees with us. We form God in our own image. If we don't think there should be judgment, then the god of wood and stone doesn't either. The god of wood and stone just wants everyone to be a good person, regardless of belief. The god of wood and stone says there is no hell, and everybody eventually goes to heaven. If we don't like a particular scriptural doctrine, then the god of wood and stone agrees with us. If we are offended by a Scriptural passage, then the god of wood and stone says it's OK, that passage doesn't really mean what it says anyway. In short, whatever belief system suits us personally, the god of wood and stone thinks that's perfectly all right too!

So no, we do not do well at all being angry at God. Rather we need to humble ourselves and remember Proverbs 1:8, "The fear of the Lord is the beginning of knowledge, but fools despise wisdom and discipline." Because, worse than Jonah, we are a very arrogant people, and we must learn that we do well to seek God's face and understand who He is rather than being angry with Him.

Discussion Questions

1. What defines a true prophet of God? Aside from God Himself, who did true prophets typically serve? How many were there at one time?
2. What were prophecies from God usually about? To whom were they directed?
3. In Jonah chapter 2:1–9, Jonah's prayer, what do you believe Jonah was describing?
4. What were the characteristics of Jonah's prayer?
5. What was God's ultimate message to Jonah? (Hint: see the last two verses of Jonah.)
6. Do we "have any right" (NIV) to be angry at God? Why or why not?

Chapter 2:

ON GRACE AND REDEMPTION

(The Book of Ruth)

1. INTRODUCTION

During the age of the Judges in Israel, 1350–1000 BC, when chaos, lawlessness, violence, and godlessness of all sorts reigned in and around the Nation of Israel, which had only entered the Promised Land some fifty years before, the Book of Ruth tells a story of devotion to God, obedience to God's laws, mercy, and redemption.[20] The Book of Ruth stands in stark contrast to the biblical accounts surrounding it describing the many acts of disastrous disobedience and apostasy committed by the Israelites, both before and after their entry into Canaan. In the Book of Ruth almost everyone does everything right. God's rules are followed, His Laws are kept and, most importantly, the people in the story display a heart for God. We will explore the themes set out in the Book of Ruth, which displays not only obedience to God, but also the virtues of having a

---

[20] John W. Reed, *The Bible Knowledge Commentary*, John F. Walvoord and Roy B. Zuck, Editors (Colorado Springs: David C. Cook, 1984) 415 et seq.

worshipful heart, a heart of gratitude, and love for the steadfast God of grace.

2. HISTORICAL BACKGROUND

Since Ruth was the great-grandmother of David, as mentioned in Ruth chapter 4:18–22, and we know David was born around 1030 BC, the events depicted in Ruth must have taken place late in the period of the judges, from around 1380 to 1050 BC.[21] The period of the judges in Israel was a chaotic and anarchic period of time when "every man did what was right in his own eyes" (Judges 17:6). The writing of the Book of Ruth has been dated from 1000 BC, during the reign of David, to times much later and even after the return of Israel from Babylonian captivity, circa 500 BC. As the last few verses of the book, cited above, trace Ruth and Boaz' lineage only to King David, and not farther on to Solomon, it seems likely that Ruth was written during the reign of David, between 1010 and 970 BC.[22]

No one knows who wrote Ruth, although Samuel is probably a good guess. Some commentators see Samuel's style in parts of the Book of Ruth and suggest Samuel or another prophet wrote Ruth, since Old Testament prophets, generally, were consistent in writing down both prophecy and history.[23]

---

[21] Charles Caldwell Ryrie, *The Ryrie Study Bible, Expanded Edition, NIV* (Chicago: Moody Press, 1994) 391

[22] Reed, Ibid., 415

[23] Eugene H. Merrill, Mark F. Rooker, and Michael A. Grisanti, *The World and the Word* (Nashville: B&H Academic, 2011) 300 et seq.

3. Prevailing Conditions

The story of Ruth begins in Bethlehem, a suburb of Jerusalem, during a famine. The famine caused Elimelech and his wife, Naomi, to go to Moab, a distance of some fifty miles, seeking better conditions. Some commentators regard the move by Elimilech as an act of disobedience to God, and thus the beginning of Naomi's trouble, as we shall see.[24] About ten years later, after Elimelech and both his sons died, his wife, Naomi, was stranded about fifty miles from Bethlehem, with no means of support and with her two now widowed daughters-in-law. When Naomi decided to return to her home in Bethlehem she was faced with the harsh and brutish conditions of the time and a trip of fifty miles, alone and without support or protection.

4. Main Characters

The main characters in the story are Naomi, the widow of Elimilech and the mother-in-law of the title character, Ruth. Ruth is Naomi's also-widowed daughter-in-law. And finally, there is Boaz, a successful and apparently unmarried farmer, honorable man of God, "man of standing" (Chapter 2:1), and eventual *go'el* (kinsman-redeemer). One focus of this chapter will especially be on Naomi. One of the important points of the chapter will be to characterize Naomi as being the driving force of the narrative and providing some of the pivotal lessons of the book.

---

[24] Reed, Ibid., 419

5. Argument

There are at least two arguments that span the entire book, and perhaps the entire Scripture. The first is the concept of redemption through God's grace, provided to all of us if, as Naomi apparently did, we humble ourselves, turn from our wicked ways, pray, and seek God's face (2 Chron. 7:14). In the book, all three main characters are, in one fashion or another, redeemed. Naomi was redeemed from desperate poverty and received the family she had always wanted. Ruth, in much the same way, was redeemed by Boaz from loneliness and poverty, finding both a good husband and a family, and became an important figure in the lineage of David, and therefore Jesus. Boaz found as loyal and kind a wife as can be and, apparently, one that was quite fond of him, and was redeemed from having his lineage die off at his death. This was all provided by God's grace in working His plan through His faithful people.

The second argument would also be an idea that permeates the book, and that is the concept of kindness (*hesed or chesed*).[25] Sometimes interpreted as *mercy*, the interpretation that also fits the Book of Ruth well is *steadfast love and devotion*. Steadfast devotion was shown first to God by Ruth. Ruth, who left her own people and went to Bethlehem with Naomi, perfectly showed that concept. Ruth was devoted, first, to God, then to Naomi and Boaz.

Another argument that also spans the entire Scripture is that, whether we can see it or not, whether things look good or things look grim, whether it seems as if nothing is going to ever work out for the better, God is still in control and driving

---

[25] James Strong, *The New Strong's Expanded Exhaustive Concordance of the Bible* (Nashville: Thomas Nelson, 2010) 93

history. On her long trip back to Bethlehem, it was a sure thing that Naomi was convinced that poverty and desperation were the only things she and Ruth had to look forward to.

6. Purpose

The purpose intended by the author, and one that would have been clearly understood by readers at the time, was that obedience to Mosaic Law in both the letter and in the heart, love of God, and godly treatment of one's fellow man, would lead to great blessing. Disobedience and sin, such as Elimelech's, would lead to disaster, not only for the individual, but for the entire family.

7. Key Verse

The key verses are Ruth 1:16–17, which will be dealt with as a poem in the exegesis section of this chapter. Ruth, in her entreaty and vow to Naomi, encompassed all of the major arguments of the book, played out simply by a woman being both obedient and loyally devoted to her God and being kind to other people.

8. Major Themes

Generally, the Book of Ruth could be summed up in four points:

1.   Everyone obeys God's Laws.
2.   Everyone is selfless.
3.   Everyone did their part.
4.   God's plan for Naomi, Boaz, and especially Ruth, to be an important part of David's lineage (and therefore Jesus'

lineage), was completed. This is what Frank Gaebelin calls "the hidden causality of God."[26]

Important themes that will be explored include:

1. **Redemption.** It is my opinion that this is the predominant theme of the whole book. Ruth is redeemed. Boaz, who apparently did not have a wife, family, or no heirs, was redeemed (so to speak). And, significantly, a main theme of the book seems to be that Naomi was redeemed.

2. **Protection** (also including "covering"). Tied in closely with the concept of redemption is the concept of being covered or protected. God protected Naomi, Ruth, and, in a sense, Boaz.

3. *Hesed,* or *checed,* used twice in Ruth, at 2:20 and 3:10, means loyalty or grace, but particularly kindness. The connotations of the term are also mercy, loving kindness, and a definition I believe is particularly on point, steadfast devotion. Kindness and steadfast devotion, both to others and to God, abounds in this book.

INTERPRETATION AND EXPOSITION

1. **Naomi's plight (Ruth 1:1–5):** The Book of Ruth opens with an introduction and background, setting the scene of the story and the desperate plight of Naomi, mother-in-law of Ruth, the namesake of the book. Some commentaries believe the story occurred during the time of the Judge, Gideon (1148–1108 BC,

---

[26] Gaebelin, Frank E., Editor, *The Expositor's Bible Commentary* (Grand Rapids: Zondervan, 1992)

Judges 6:1–8:28).[27] Naomi and her husband, Elimelech, lived in Bethlehem (of Judea). As the result of a famine in Judea, Elimelech decided to move to Moab, located on the East side of the Jordan River, about fifty miles away. It is suggested that this may have been the act of disobedience to God that caused disaster to fall on Naomi, that is, abandoning the land God gave them and their accompanying lack of faith.[28] In addition, both of Elimelech's sons married Moabite women, Ruth and Orpah, and they remained in Moab for ten years. God also cautioned against commingling with the pagans and marriage to pagan women, and the Moabites were certainly pagan (Numbers 22:1–25:18). Perhaps as a result, Elimelech and both sons died, and Ruth was left destitute, with two Moabite daughters-in-law. They lived in Moab for ten years, which seems more than enough time for Elimelech and his sons to have formed a syncretistic religion with the pagan Moabites and been assimilated into the population. Nonetheless, Naomi seemed to have remained a devout Jew. She decided to leave and go home to Bethlehem as soon as she found out that there was no more famine there.

2. Her daughters' decisions and Naomi's long journey (Ruth 1:6–14): Naomi began her fifty-mile journey home to Bethlehem with her two daughters-in-law. Apparently, at the beginning of the journey, Naomi made a decision, which was not in her best interest, but one that she felt would be best for the two girls. She decided to send them back to their families. Naomi was already destitute and desperate, and allowing the two women

---

[27] John W. Reed, *Ibid.,* 418

[28] Victor P. Hamilton, *Handbook on the Historical Books* (Grand Rapids: Baker Academic, 2001) 190-191

Frank E. Gaebelein, *The Expositors Bible Commentary* (Grand Rapids: Zondervan, 1992) 520

to come along would make matters even worse, because Naomi could neither support herself nor protect herself on the dangerous journey back home, much less her two daughters-in-law. Naomi, who thought she was acting in the best interest of the girls, would have to make the trip completely alone. Naomi blessed the girls (*chesed* or *hesed* – God's grace and kindness on them)[29] and tried to send them home. At first, they both refused. Naomi argued that they have no better future in Judah than she did, but some chance of a better life in Moab. Finally, Orpah obeyed Naomi and turned back. This was probably the standard and correct behavior when ordered to do something by one's parents. But Ruth was not dissuaded and "clung" to Naomi, refusing to leave.

3. Ruth's poem of devotion (Ruth 1:15–18): This begins Ruth's well-known response and final plea to Naomi, which is considered the literary highlight of the book, and deservedly so. Ruth's response was actually a vow to both Naomi and God. Tod Linafelt makes a good case that Ruth's final response to Naomi was actually in poetic form,[30] with a series of four doublets:

> "And Ruth said,
> Do not press me to leave you,
> Or to turn back from you.
> For wherever you go, I will go,
> And wherever you stay, I will stay.
> Your people shall be my people,
> And your God shall be my God.

---

[29] James Strong, Ibid., 93

[30] Tod Linafelt, "Narrative and Poetic Art in the Book of Ruth", *Journal of Bible and Theology*, 64, no. 2 (April 2010) 117-129

Wherever you die, I will die,
And there I will be buried.
Thus may the Lord do to me and more, if anything
but death separates me from you."

Linafelt goes on to point out the significance of the fact that this oration by Ruth can be seen as a poem. Linafelt holds that, in the Scriptures, when something said by someone is in poetic form it indicates that what is being said comes straight from the heart of the individual saying it and expresses that individual's true feelings and beliefs.[31] It is clear here that Ruth, even though a Moabite, has somehow become a devout believer in God, as has Naomi, as we shall see. Not only is the poem a promise, or vow, to Naomi, but is also, and maybe more importantly, a vow to God.

In Chapter 1:18, Naomi saw that Ruth was going to go along regardless, and maybe also saw that Ruth was truly a God-fearing and obedient servant of God, and didn't want to go back to living among the pagan and detestable Moabites. Ruth was a true convert to Judaism.[32] As we shall see, being a Moabite woman didn't seem to be an obstacle to God so long as she believed and obeyed. So, Naomi relented and let Ruth come along.

4. Naomi's lament (Ruth 1:19-21): Naomi and Ruth arrive in Bethlehem. Bethlehem is probably a small place, where everyone knew everything that was happening, so Naomi's

---

[31] Ibid.

[32] Robert Goldenberg, "How Did Ruth Become a Model Convert", *Conservative Judaism*, 61, no. 3 (Spring 2010)

arrival after ten years caused quite a stir.[33] But Naomi told the women who greeted her to change her name from Naomi, meaning "pleasant," to Mara, meaning "bitter," because "the Lord has afflicted me, the Almighty has brought misfortune upon me." Naomi said she left "full," but the Lord brought her back "empty." Naomi lost everything that had any meaning to the Jews of her time. She had lost her family and thereby any hope of a lineage and descendants. She lost any chance of security and safety, and she lost all her possessions and wealth, with no chance of getting any of it back. In short, there was no hope left for her. As John Reed states, "She saw nothing ahead but the loneliness, abandonment, and helplessness of widowhood."[34] What Naomi says in this statement reflects the Jewish belief at the time that God blessed the righteous and brought disaster on the disobedient. It does not appear, however, that Naomi was complaining to God about her treatment. She seemed to be aware of the nature and cause of her disaster. The key was her faith. Her belief and devotion to God didn't seem to be affected by her fate. Neither had Ruth's faith been affected, as pointed out a few verses previous in the poem. At this point, the story has reached the low point for Naomi, but the two women seem determined to move forward in steadfast devotion to God.

5. The barley harvest (Ruth 1:22): The last verse of the chapter sets the stage for the next two chapters simply by saying that the two women arrived in Bethlehem in April, at the beginning of the barley harvest. The barley harvest lasted about six weeks, which gave the women a chance to glean the harvested

---

[33] J. Hardee Kennedy, *The Broadman Bible Commentary* – Ruth (Nashville: Broadman Press, 1970) 470

[34] Reed, Ibid., 421

fields and at least feed themselves. This is in accordance with the Mosaic Law, where God provides for the destitute by allowing gleaning (Lev. 19:9–10, 23:22).

6. Ruth gleans and meets Boaz (Ruth 2:1–7): Naomi and Ruth found themselves in a situation in which it would be easy to lose all hope. Without support of any kind, and with no apparent chance at a better life, Naomi already styled her life as "bitter" (Chapter 1:20). Hope arrived in chapter two with the intro-duction, by the narrator, of Boaz (Chapter 2:1) as a relative of Naomi's husband and a man of "standing." We only find out later that Naomi was keenly aware of who Boaz was, and that he was a relative of Naomi's deceased husband (Chapter 3:2). The term "man of standing" means "mighty man of valor"[35] and "mighty man of wealth,"[36] and suggests that Boaz was a promi-nent and well-respected member of the community and led an exemplary lifestyle.[37] No mention is made in the Book of Ruth as to whether Boaz was married or had a family, but the impres-sion is that he was single, with no heirs. We know that it is the beginning of the barley harvest, in April.[38] In Ruth 2:2, Ruth suggested to Naomi that Naomi let her go into the fields to reap grain. This was according to the Mosaic Law (Lev. 19:9, 23:22), with which Naomi surely was familiar and with which we learn that Ruth was also familiar. Gleaning, as provided by the Law, allowed the poor and destitute to follow the harvesters and pick up grain that had been dropped. In fact, the Law provided for gleaners by specifying that harvesters not pick up grain that

---

[35] Reed, *Ibid.*, 422

[36] Strong, Ibid., 15

[37] Reed, Ibid., 422

[38] Ryrie, Ibid., 393

was dropped and actually purposely leave some (Dt. 24:19–21). Here God's concern for the poor and destitute leaves a very clear message in the Law. We also see this message, a message of kindness, later in the actions of Boaz. Ruth soon "finds herself" gleaning in the fields of Boaz. John Reed doesn't believe this was by accident.[39] Ryrie disagrees, saying this was through the "providence of God."[40] While either one could be the case, one suspects that Naomi, who drives the entire book of Ruth, may have suggested Ruth try Boaz's fields first. (Naomi's honest and principled motivation becomes clear in Ruth 3:1–2.) As Ruth gleaned, Boaz appeared, greeted his men, and inquired as to who Ruth was. He had apparently already noticed her (Ruth 2:4–5). Boaz was informed that Ruth was the Moabite woman who returned with Naomi, and had steadily worked in the fields with only a short rest. To this point, it has been mentioned several times that Ruth was a Moabite woman. The Moabites were a Semitic people but not Jews (Hebrews). The Moabites were descended from Moab, the son of Lot, by Lot's eldest daughter, who seduced the drunken Lot (Gen. 19:36–37). The Moabites were pagans. While there was a proscription against marrying a Canaanite woman (Deut. 7), no such restriction existed against marrying a Moabite woman. Obviously, Ruth was a believer in God, not a pagan. Finally, commentators note the greeting of Boaz to his men, their response, and Boaz's blessing to Ruth as demonstrating good leadership, devotion to his men, and Boaz's "nobility of character and devout quality of his religious faith."[41]

---

[39] Ibid., 422

[40] Ryrie, Ibid., 394

[41] Kennedy, Ibid., 472

7. Boaz shows great kindness to Ruth (Ruth 2:8–13): Boaz knew who Ruth was and what she had done and was doing for Naomi. He invited her to glean alongside his own servant girls, in safety, and use the water drawn by his men. Boaz showed uncommon kindness above and beyond the requirements of the Law. Ruth then bowed and asked why she had been shown such favor. Boaz's response sets one of the themes of the book. He said he knew the kindness and devotion Ruth had shown to Naomi, blessed Ruth, asked the Lord to reward her kindness, and then stated, "under whose wings (God's) you have come to take refuge" (Chapter 2:12). The idea of being covered by wings appears several times in Scripture, both in the Psalms and, most notably, in Matthew 23:37, where Jesus says, regarding the Jews corporately, "How often I have longed to gather your children together, as a hen gathers her chicks under her wings." This imagery speaks strongly of God's constant protection and rescue from the perils of life. It also reflects both the Old Testament and New Testament grace that God provides for us every day. In Chapter 2:13, Ruth thanked Boaz and then demonstrated those themes again by stating she didn't even have the standing of Boaz' servant girls. Ruth was really expressing her gratitude for the protection and for the grace (unmerited favor) she received from both Boaz and God.

8. Boaz favors Ruth again (Ruth 2:14–16): At mealtime, Boaz not only made sure Ruth was fed well, but also gave instructions to his men to make sure Ruth found plenty of grain to glean. Boaz didn't have to do any of that for Ruth. This continues the themes of kindness, protection, rescue from peril, and grace. There is a strong, and remarkable parallel here between these Old Testament themes, written around 1000 BC, and the salvation themes of the New Testament, written one thousand years later. God doesn't change. His grace, protection, and redemption remain the same.

9. Ruth reports to Naomi (Ruth 1:17–23): Ruth returned home, not only with an unusually large amount of grain, but the leftovers from her meal with Boaz and his men. Naomi noticed immediately that Ruth found favor with someone and asked her where she gleaned. When Naomi learned that Ruth worked in the fields of Boaz, we can see joy appear in Naomi. Naomi blessed Boaz and made it clear that Boaz had always been a kind man and had not changed. Naomi begins to drive the Book of Ruth once more by stating that "He is one of our kinsman-redeemers." The Hebrew word for the kinsman-redeemer is *go'el*.[42] The concept of the *go'el* is based on Deuteronomy 25:5–10, which specifies that the kinsman-redeemer had the responsibility to buy back (redeem) family property being sold out of the family, and marry a childless widow to carry on the family name (called the Law of levirate marriage).[43] We have already seen that Boaz was a kinsmen of Naomi's husband. Here Naomi, and probably Ruth, clearly understand the blessings God gave them in their desperate need. Again, very much like New Testament theology, God rescues, redeems, and blesses us in our darkest hour. The chapter concludes with Naomi advising Ruth to accept Boaz' request to spend the rest of the harvest season safe and protected (covered) gleaning Boaz' fields. Ryrie states Ruth probably spent about six weeks working in the fields of Boaz.[44]

---

[42] Hamilton, Ibid., 195

[43] Ryrie, Ibid., 396

[44] Ibid., 395

10. Naomi forms a desperate plan and Ruth agrees (Ruth 3:1-5) Ruth has now spent six weeks in the fields of Boaz, gleaning grain for her and Naomi to survive.[45] Due to the kindness of Boaz, Ruth was even allowed to glean along with Boaz' own servant girls. The harvest finished and the grain was stored on the threshing floor (Ruth 2:23-3:3). Because of the abruptness of the events that take place in the third chapter, it seems to be understood that Boaz took a liking to Ruth, and Boaz was also aware that he was kin to Naomi and in line as a kinsman-redeemer. At any rate, at the beginning of chapter three, Naomi, still feeling the threat of impending disaster (Mark Dever states, "She is also destined to be alone, and therefore ruin and destitution will always threaten to overtake her.")[46], decides that what seems to be something of a desperate and bold act is in order. The opportunity presents itself because Boaz and his men would spend the night on the threshing floor with the grain (Chapter 3:2-3). Naomi appealed to Ruth by saying that she wanted to try to "find a home" for Ruth (Chapter 3:1). Euphemistically, this means finding a husband for Ruth. The remainder of Naomi's plan included a cleaned up and perfumed Ruth in her best clothes and a late-night trip down to the threshing floor, which had to be done in secrecy for the benefit of everyone's reputation. Ruth's statement, "I will do whatever you say" (Ruth 3:5) indicates Ruth agreed with Naomi that that was God's plan, and not exclusively Naomi's, since Ruth refused to obey Naomi and go home to her family in Moab to begin with, probably because she thought it was against God's will. What appears to be the idea here, and it seems a desperate one, is to get Boaz to redeem

---

[45] Ryrie, Ibid., 395

[46] Mark Dever, *The Message of the Old Testament* (Wheaton: Crossway Books, 2006) 234

both Naomi's family property and also take Ruth as his wife. Presumably Ruth understood that.

11. Ruth successfully executes the plan (Ruth 3:6–13): This begins the execution of Naomi's plan by Ruth. What happens seems very odd by twenty-first century standards. After Boaz finished "eating and drinking and was in good spirits" (Chapter 3: 7) he went to bed behind the grain pile and fell fast asleep. Ruth, apparently incognito in a cloak, slipped in and "uncovered his feet" (Chapter 3:7) and laid down. Boaz woke up in the middle of the night and was apparently startled to find a woman laying at his feet, because he asked, "Who are you?" (Chapter 3:9). Then, in verse 9, Ruth proposed that Boaz take on the responsibility of both marriage to her and the redemption of Naomi's property, all in accordance with the Laws of Moses and levirate marriage (Deut. 25:5–10). Apparently, it was customarily the widowed woman's responsibility to make this proposition, not the man's.[47] To accomplish all of this, Ruth simply said, "Spread the corner of your garment over me, since you are a kinsman-redeemer." (Ruth 3:9) This phrase is odd to us, but would not have been to Boaz. Boaz would have understood this to be a request for Boaz to act as *go'el* and a proposal of levirate marriage.[48]

Boaz's response to all of this begins in verse 10. His response revealed the fact that Boaz was perhaps much older than Ruth, apparently childless, and had likely given up finding a bride of childbearing age. He blessed Ruth, said *her* kindness shown to him was even greater than the kindness she had shown to Naomi, and agreed to all she asked. The deal was made. One

---

[47] Dever, Ibid., 236

[48] Ryrie, Ibid., 396

thing that appears striking in this episode is the fact that Boaz believes it is Ruth who is kind to him, not the reverse. His unselfish attitude is remarkable, both then and now.

It is also important for the full understanding of this passage to note that the word for "garment" used by Ruth is the same word, translated "wing," used by Boaz in Ruth 2:12, when he said to Ruth, "May you be richly rewarded by the Lord, the God of Israel, under whose *wings* you have come to take refuge."[49] Any notion that Ruth seduced Boaz, which may occur to a modern reader of chapter three, is completely without foundation in light of the actual meaning of what took place, that meaning being one of protection and redemption.

12. Ruth reports to Naomi (Ruth 3:14–18): The chapter closes with Ruth returning to Naomi, in the morning and unseen, and bringing with her a bunch of grain given as a token by Boaz. Naomi closes the chapter by assuring Ruth, who is apparently anxious regarding her acceptance by Boaz, that Boaz is a man of such character that he will not rest until the deal is closed.

13. Boaz acts as *goʾel* and closes the deal (Ruth 4:1–6): As Naomi said at the end of chapter 3, Boaz would not rest that day until the matter of redemption, all in accordance with the law, was settled. Boaz set out to the main gate of the city, where business was conducted, to find the nearest kinsman of Naomi (It seems Boaz was second in line). In the matter of the redemption of the land and the levirate marriage of Ruth, the commentators, except for Ryrie, seem to agree.[50] The majority is of the

---

49 Kennedy, Ibid., 475, Gaebelin, Ibid., 537

50 Dever, Ibid., 237, Kennedy, Ibid., 476, Gaebelein, Ibid., 541, Reed, Ibid., 426, Hamilton, Ibid., 199

opinion that Naomi herself was being forced to sell the property she inherited at Elimelech's death to have money to live on and because she could not work the land herself.[51] This would result in the land being sold out of the family line, a situation not in keeping with the Laws of Moses because it would lead Naomi and Ruth into a downward spiral of abject poverty.[52] Therefore, the *go'el* was obligated to purchase the property to keep it in the family line and, in essence, prevent Naomi and Ruth from becoming destitute (Deut. 25:5–10).

Taking the opinion of Ryrie,[53] this seems to be the situation: The land of Elimelech was apparently sold out of the family when Elimelech moved to Moab. According to the Mosaic Law of redemption, that land may be redeemed or purchased back into the family by a kinsman of Elimelech. Then, by inheritance, the land would first belong to Naomi and then Ruth, as Naomi's surviving daughter-in-law. Therefore, whoever redeemed the land was obligated to take Ruth in levirate marriage to ensure the land was passed down to the right family. However, the text itself indicates that Naomi herself was selling the property (Ruth 4:3).

Boaz explained the situation to the next-of-kin, who he met at the city gate. While the kinsman was willing to redeem the land he was not willing to marry Ruth, probably because the land would pass down to Ruth's children when he died, not to the ones he already had.

14. The deal is sealed (Ruth 4:7–12): The nearest kinsman told Boaz that he could not redeem the land and marry Ruth also

---

[51] Ibid.

[52] Ibid.

[53] Ryrie, Ibid., 396

and took off his sandal, indicating that Boaz was the lawful kinsman-redeemer (Ruth 4:8). Chapter 4: 11-12 reflect the responses of the elders at the gate who were witnesses to the transaction between Boaz and the other kinsman. Boaz was offered a great blessing by the elders; that of many children, represented by Rachel and Leah, wives of Jacob, who between them had twelve sons who were the fathers of the twelve tribes of Israel. That was apparently the biggest blessing they could give Boaz and Ruth. It indicates that, as a man in good standing, Boaz was lacking only one thing—children to carry his name.

15. Epilogue part one (Ruth 4:13–17): This section begins what we might call the epilogue of the story, or "how it all came out in the end." To the great joy of Naomi, God allowed Boaz and Ruth, who had been childless up to that point, to have a son, who was named Obed (Chapter 4:13). The "Greek chorus" of women echoes this joy in Chapter 4: 15, "He will renew your life and sustain you in your old age." Naomi had gone, in just four chapters, from a hopeless situation to a state of complete fulfillment and joy. For pulling off Naomi's desperate plan, and then having a son, Ruth was also highly praised by the women. The narrative closes with Naomi, a proud grandparent, holding Obed on her lap.

16. Epilogue part two (Ruth 4:18–22): In the last verses of the book a lineage is added. This is the ironic twist, or the surprise ending to the story. It seems all along we have been reading about the lineage of King David, and therefore Jesus. It turns out that Ruth, not even an ethnic Jew, and Boaz, are King David's great grandparents. God drives history.

Application

The original readers of the story would surely have appreciated the fact that the people involved, Naomi, Ruth, and Boaz, were obedient to God and obeyed His laws and were therefore blessed by prosperity, family, and being in the line of David. Since it was probably written during the reign of David, The Book of Ruth would have also given the original readers an insight into David's heritage and some evidence that David was God's anointed and not just the people's choice, as Saul was.

Readers then, and now, can understand the moral lessons of the Book of Ruth, in both the Old Testament sense of complying with the Mosaic Law and having a heart for God, and the New Testament sense of loving others and treating them the way we would want to be treated. Paul said to "keep in step with the Spirit" by displaying the fruit of the Spirit which includes, among others, kindness, goodness, faithfulness, and self-control, and particularly in the Book of Ruth, kindness (Gal. 5:22–26). In both cases, God honors the display of these Christ-like virtues with blessing, for us and everyone around us. Surely both original and modern readers can understand the simple statement from Hosea 6:8, which states, "For I desire mercy, not sacrifice." The term "mercy", *hesed,* means both the faithful love of God and the steadfast devotion of His people to Him. This message was likely part of the author's intent and is one that readers three thousand years ago and today can both understand.

A common overall theme in many of the books of the Bible, and a strong theme in Ruth, is the lesson that disobeying God leads to disaster and obedience leads to blessing. "Walking always in God's ways" is highly emphasized in this story. After the disaster that befell Naomi, who was simply following her ill-fated husband, everyone in the story obeyed the Mosaic Law as best they understood it. Everyone acted in a selfless fashion. Everyone did their part in bringing about the proper conclusion to the events. God helps and God guides. Ruth is a micro-example of the way both the society of the Ancient Jews and our society *should* work. It is one of the very few stories in the Old Testament that has a happy ending. The reason would have been clear to readers then and should be clear to readers now: Try to walk in God's ways and He will help you. Disobey and you will face disaster sooner or later.

The theme of redemption runs all the way through the Book of Ruth. Ruth, a widow from another culture, but a follower of God, finds redemption in an unexpected husband, children, and family. Boaz finds unexpected redemption and joy in the apparent devotion of Ruth to him and fulfillment of his lineage. But redemption falls particularly on Naomi. The book begins and ends with scenes involving Naomi. In the first scene (Ruth 1:1–5) Naomi was despondent. She lost everything that a Jew of the time could have in life. She lost her husband, her means of support and security, and her sons. She was alone in a foreign, pagan, and probably somewhat hostile, land. She was about as lost as a soul can get. In Ruth Chapter 1:20 Naomi even says, "The Almighty has made my life very bitter," and "The Lord has afflicted me; the Almighty has brought misfortune upon me." But, while Naomi was hurt bad, she was still loyally focused on God. It has been said that, while we can question things that go on in this world, we should ask the questions of God. Naomi seemed to do just that. Naomi drove the narrative, suggesting that Ruth go glean (and probably whose fields she should try first) and how she should act (Ruth Chapter2:22), and by proposing that Ruth should take a daring risk, which makes up the climactic moment in the book. Naomi winds up at the end completely redeemed by God from her disaster, with her grandchild,

Obed, on her lap. Audiences then and now can surely understand that Naomi went from being a throw-away of society to
being redeemed through her devotion, obedience, and reli-
ance on God.

Finally, there is a clear parallel and important message in
the theme of redemption between Old Testament theology and
the Church Age under Jesus. In the Old Testament, as here in
the Book of Ruth, obedience to the Mosaic Law and devotion
to God were paramount. In the New Testament, Jesus came
to fulfill (meaning to "complete" or "finish") the Mosaic Law
and therefore offer salvation to everyone who believes, Jew and
Gentile alike. But the message is that God never changes. The
God of Ruth shows the same grace and redemption as the God
who sent Jesus. The same attributes of God appear consistent
and unchanging throughout both Testaments. The systems
change, but God remains the same. His requirements are the
same: faith, steadfast devotion, obedience, acting as God wants
us to act, and doing things God's way. Naomi, Ruth, and Boaz all
display these virtues and God blessed them. These same virtues
are reflected in the life and teaching of Jesus and throughout the
New Testament and are still the virtues God wants us to hold in
both our heads and our hearts.

DISCUSSION QUESTIONS

1. What exactly was Elimelech's sin?
2. In Matthew 23:37 Jesus used the term "wings" in much the
   same manner as Ruth and Boaz both did (Ruth 3:9 and Ruth
   2:12). Discuss the idea of God covering us with His wings.
3. The Hebrew term *hesed*, typically translated to "mercy," has
   a much broader and more profound meaning than simple
   mercy. Discuss some of the applications of the term *hesed*.

Chapter 3:

ON PRAYER

INTRODUCTION

The intent of this chapter is to use Nehemiah 1:5–11 to demonstrate what God has shown us in the Scriptures concerning the efficacy, necessity, proper attitude, and proper action as it relates to prayer. Nehemiah's prayer, given some 2,500 years ago and faithfully recorded and preserved in the Old Testament, serves not only as an Old Testament model for prayer, but a template of sorts even today for the condition of both our heart and our head when we face God and truly pray.

So often in our society and culture, particularly when people face hard times, when they need help badly, or, increasingly, when a disaster occurs, a public figure wishes to appear religious and invoke the Almighty, so a public prayer is dashed off, which typically runs along the lines of "We have gotten ourselves in deep trouble God" so come "heal our land" (2 Chron. 7:14).

Certainly, Nehemiah was a public figure, and he was in the process of attempting to save his people. His prayer is one that involves not just Nehemiah, but his whole family and all remaining Jews at that time. But we will see that God requires a lot more from us when we pray than just a request for help in time of need.

The Context

To understand The Book of Nehemiah, his prayer, and Nehemiah himself, it is helpful to first go back to the events set out in 2 Chronicles. The Jewish nation existed in Palestine, "Eretz Yisrael," the land given to them by God, since about 1400 BC, after their return from captivity in Egypt.[54]The Scriptures set out basic covenants given by God to the Jews involving the promise of a nation, the promise of land, the promise of a national redemption, the promise of many descendants, and the promise of a Messiah (Gen. 12:1–3, 2 Samuel Ch. 7 and Jer. 31:31–34).[55] The Jews, therefore, as the chosen people of God, had (and still have) a covenant relationship with Him. On the one hand, God wishes to redeem His people. On the other hand, God wants His people to worship, follow, trust, and obey Him. This they failed to do on several occasions.

We find, in 2 Chronicles, a Jewish Nation in exile, having been overcome by the Babylonians in 586 BC. Prior to that exile, King Josiah, ruler of Israel from 640 to 609, found his people deep in apostasy involving Baal worship and a general disregard of God and the Scriptures. It is recorded that Josiah even recovered the Torah from the temple, where it had apparently been abandoned (2 Chron. 34:14–21). Josiah restored the worship of God in Israel. "He did what was right in the eyes of the Lord.... not turning aside to the right or to the left" (2 Chron. 34:1–2). But after Josiah was killed in battle, Judah once again turned

---

[54] Eugene H. Merrill, Mark F. Rooker, and Michael A. Grisanti. *The World and The Word*. Nashville: B&H Publishing Group, 2011

[55] Ryrie, Charles Caldwell. *The Ryrie Study Bible*, KJV. Chicago: Moody Press, 1976, 1978

away from God. The last recorded king of Judea was Zedekiah.[56] Because the king and his people turned away from God and apparently returned to Baal worship, God allowed the nation to be destroyed by Nebuchadnezzar of Babylon in 586 BC, and about fifty thousand Jews were taken into exile in Babylon. This fulfilled a prophecy of Jeremiah (Jer. 13:20–27).

In 538 BC the Babylonians were conquered by Cyrus (The Great) of Persia. Cyrus then freed the captive Jews, to return to their homeland. This also fulfilled a prophecy of Jeremiah (2 Chron. 36:22). In addition, Cyrus returned gold and silver objects plundered from the temple in Jerusalem by Nebuchadnezzar, and ordered the returning Jews to rebuild the temple, or at least approved the rebuilding of it (Ezra 1).[57]

The return from exile and the rebuilding began, but not without opposition, particularly from the Samaritans, who had remained in Judea during the exile. In addition, parts of Judea had been overrun by the Samaritans to the north, the Idumaeans to the south, and the Philistines to the west. These groups had intermarried with Jews who remained in Judea during the exile and practiced some form of Baal worship or, as Ryrie states, a "syncretistic religion." None of the groups wanted to see the Jews return under the favor of the Persian king, and all wished the effort to rebuild Jerusalem to fail. And fail it did to the point where Nehemiah, a Jewish member of the court of the Persian king, now Artaxerxes I, heard about the deep trouble his people were in.[58]

---

[56] Ibid., 2 Kings

[57] Yamauchi, Edwin *The Expositor's Bible Commentary – Nehemiah*. Grand Rapids: Zondervan, 1988

[58] Merrill *World and Word*. 343 - 353

A word must be said about Artaxerxes I (and about kings in general). While Artaxerxes appears to be somewhat agreeable in Nehemiah (Neh. 2:1–10), the historical accounts color that image somewhat. Artaxerxes I, who ruled from 461 to 424 BC, took the throne after his father, Xerxes, was murdered by a court official. Not only did Artaxerxes manage to kill the court official, but he also killed one of his own brothers, Darius. He then defeated his other brother in battle to take the throne. Artaxerxes was eighteen years old. Being king may have been good, but it was also dark and dangerous. It is clear from all historical accounts, most notably the account of The Battle of Thermopylae (480 BC) waged between Xerxes and the Greeks, that kings of Persia had life-and-death power over everyone and everything in their realm. They were not nice guys, and dealing with them was a very dangerous undertaking.[59] Ryrie states that the Persians were, at the time, noted for having a complete disdain for human life[60] (pg. 736, intro to Esther, NIV).

A word must also be said about Baal worship. Baal was a typical Canaanite pagan god who emerged from a pantheon of various other gods and goddesses. He was important to the various groups surrounding Judea because they thought he brought rain for the crops to grow in a very dry area and was also the god of fertility. There were temples and priests dedicated to Baal worship, complete with all manners of barbaric ritual, including human sacrifice and temple prostitution. Why this phony religion was so compelling to the ancient Jews is a mystery to me, but there are many instances where the Jewish

---

[59] Ibid., 15

[60] Ryrie *Study Bible.* 743

nation slipped into apostasy and intermarried with Baal worshipers. This was the case that confronted Nehemiah.[61]

It is generally agreed that Nehemiah was likely written by Nehemiah himself, perhaps in a set of personal journals, and compiled by Ezra. Ezra was a priest and author of the book bearing his name. He was also a very important figure in the story of Nehemiah and the Jews' return to Jerusalem. It is thought that Ezra returned from exile several years earlier than Nehemiah. A devout Jew, Ezra found, preserved, and compiled the Torah (the first five books of Moses), perhaps Chronicles, and other documents that now make up the Old Testament. While Nehemiah, as Governor of Judea, took on the rebuilding of the city wall of Jerusalem, Ezra was responsible for rebuilding the temple. Both Ezra and Nehemiah took on the task of restoring proper worship of God.[62]

Nehemiah, and the book of Nehemiah, begin in the court of Artaxerxes I in about 444–445 BC. Nehemiah, although a Jew, was "cupholder" for the king (Neh. 1:1–11). Artaxerxes I had been king for about twenty years by that time. It is not known how long Nehemiah had served Artaxerxes I, but Nehemiah was apparently a trusted and valued servant, as might be inferred from his position. A "cupholder" was a person who tasted the king's food and drink to ensure against poison.[63] This would be someone close to the king at all times and, by inference, a very trusted servant. It is clear from the passage in Nehemiah 2:2 that the king and Nehemiah were something of companions, and this may be the case simply because the king couldn't drink without Nehemiah.

---

[61] Merrill *World and Word*. 15

[62] Ryrie Study Bible. 701, 719

[63] Ryrie Study Bible. 719

As the story opens, Nehemiah receives some awful news from his brother, Hanani, regarding Jerusalem and the Jewish remnant and those returning from exile. Hanani's description included the words "great trouble" and "disgrace" (Neh. 1:3). Hanani added that Jerusalem's walls were down and had been "burned with fire" (Ibid). Some scholars state that the Jews in exile were much more devout and observant than the group that remained in Judea. This may have been because they were a foreign, captive people away from their home. To preserve their identity as a unique people, their religion became the only remaining element that bound them together.[64] At any rate, Nehemiah was clearly a devout Jew who feared and worshipped God. The news from his brother greatly upset him. In fact, so distraught was Nehemiah that he would risk his life to help his people (Neh. 1:4).

What Nehemiah saw, from the brief description in Nehemiah 1:1–3, was a terminal threat to the continued existence of the Jews as a people set aside by God. (Gen. 12:1–3, Ex. 19:5, and Deut. 7:6–8). It was clear to Nehemiah that, if the Jews weren't simply wiped out by their hostile neighbors, they would be absorbed through intermarriage. One way or the other, he was looking at the extinction of the Jews both religiously and physically. His people would cease to exist. Nehemiah may have seen it this way: The Jews in Jerusalem were not fully keeping God's covenants, and were not obeying and worshiping God and would, therefore, be destroyed (Ex. 19:5).

Nehemiah had decided to petition Artaxerxes to appoint him governor of Judea and allow him to go to Jerusalem for the explicit purpose of rebuilding the city walls and restoring his people to their right relationship with God.

---

[64] Yamauchi *Expositor's Bible.* 570

Meaning

This was so serious and so important in Nehemiah's heart that Nehemiah engaged in ritual fasting and mourning before he went to God in prayer. Nehemiah had also formed a plan, but one that would put him at risk of his life and could spill over to all the Jews. So, before he initiated his plan, Nehemiah sought to pray. Nehemiah 1:5–11 (NIV) states:

> O Lord, God of heaven, the great and awesome God, who keeps his covenant of love with those who love him and obey his commands, let your ear be attentive and your eyes open to hear the prayer your servant is praying before you day and night for your servants, the people of Israel. I confess the sins we Israelites, including myself and my father's house, have committed against you. We have acted very wickedly toward you. We have not obeyed the commands, decrees and laws you gave your servant Moses.
>
> Remember the instruction you gave your servant Moses, saying, If you are unfaithful, I will scatter you among the nations, but if you return to me, and obey my commands, then even if your exiled people are at the farthest horizon, I will gather them from there and bring them to the place I have chosen as a dwelling for my Name.
>
> They are your servants and your people, whom you redeemed by your great strength and your mighty hand. O Lord, let your ear be attentive to the prayer

of this your servant and to the prayer of your servants who delight in revering your name. Give your servant success today by granting him favor in the presence of this man.

To begin with, Nehemiah's prayer reflects a thorough knowledge of the Torah and subsequent books of the Old Testament, up to and including 1 and 2 Chronicles. While New Testament prayer relies on the saving grace of Jesus, Old Testament prayer was based on the covenants (promises) made by God to the Jews.[65] Some of those covenants are conditional (if you, then I) and some are not (I will). Nehemiah first invokes part of the Mosaic covenant (Ex. 19:5–6), which was conditional. The Jews were required to "obey me fully and keep my covenant" whereupon they would be "my treasured possession" (Exodus 19:5). The covenant that is referred to is that the Jews would be set aside unto God and be a "holy nation." Later, in Chapter 20, God would also present the Jews with the Ten Commandments (Ex. 20:1–17). Nehemiah's confession of disobedience likely included failure to obey the ten commandments.

Nehemiah then pleaded for mercy based on covenants made by God to restore the Jews to Jerusalem. Jeremiah 23:3 states, "I myself will gather the remnant of my flock out of all the countries where I have driven them and will bring them back to their pasture." And, again, Jeremiah 31:10 states "He who scattered Israel will gather them."

Finally, Jeremiah made his petition, to grant him success in his request to Artaxerxes. Nehemiah based his request on God's enduring love for his chosen people ("They are your servants

---

[65] Chafer, Lewis Sperry, Systematic Theology. Dallas: Dallas Theological Seminary, 1948, 1976

and your people", Nehemiah 1:10), and Nehemiah's penitence for his people's sins.

Nehemiah's prayer roughly followed both an Old Testament and New Testament form for proper prayer, one given by God (2 Chron. 7:14), and one given by Jesus (Matt. 6:6–7). Nehemiah was roughly following the requirements in 2 Chronicles in his prayer. 2 Chronicles 7:14, a familiar but often wrongly applied verse, states, "If my people, who are called by my name, will humble themselves and pray and seek my face and turn from their wicked ways, then will I hear from heaven and will forgive their sin and heal their land" (NIV).

Nehemiah likely had 2 Chronicles in mind when he offered his prayer, because he followed the requirements. He prayed. He had a petition. He asked God for something. But first, he humbled himself, his family, and the entire Jewish nation before God. He sought "God's face" i.e., he confessed his, his family's, and the nation's sins. He was repentant. He knew they had all had been wicked. Inherent in humility and repentance is the desire to do better: "turn from their wicked ways."

The Lord's Prayer is also a model (Matt. 6:9–13). It begins, as does Nehemiah's prayer, with worship, "hallowed be thy name". It requires humility, "Thy will be done on Earth". It seeks forgiveness of sins, "forgive us our trespasses". It demonstrates repentance and a change of heart, "lead us not into temptation, but deliver us from evil". And it has a petition, "give us this day our daily bread". The difference is that Christians in the Church Age are praying based on God's grace through Jesus. The Jews of the Old Testament (and now) pray based on their covenants with God.

SIGNIFICANCE

One of the most significant lessons we can learn from Nehemiah's prayer involves our attitude about prayer. Both the Old Testament and the New Testament make clear that God understands our heart, not just our minds and our acts. The Old Testament Jews repeatedly followed all of the rituals and laws but failed in that they did not love God in their heart (Deut. 6:5). Christ pointed this out many times. A good example is the passage in Matthew 6:19-21. It is well known and begins, "Do not store up for yourselves treasures on earth." It ends with, "For where your treasure is, there your *heart* will be also." Another passage, Matthew 19:14-22, involves "the rich young ruler." The man came to Jesus thinking he had kept all of the laws and commandments and wanted to know what other act he could do to work his way to heaven. He was very wealthy. Jesus told him to "Go, sell your possessions and give to the poor, and then you will have treasures in heaven." The man went away sad. Why? Because Jesus knew that, in his heart, he loved money more than God. The lesson is that prayer begins with love in our hearts for God over everything else, just as was displayed by Nehemiah.

Nehemiah's prayer also demonstrates four commonalities between Nehemiah's prayer, the Lord's Prayer, and the passage in 2 Chronicles. All of these have a great deal to do with the condition of our heart. The first is that we should approach God in a spirit of worship, acknowledging in our hearts exactly who He is and what He has done to redeem us.

The second commonality is that we should approach God in prayer with a spirit of humility. The rich young ruler was clearly not a humble man. Nehemiah was humble. We are not, generally, a humble nation. Many of us want to reach up to God and make Him a deal. Many of us want God to do it our way. We want God to be on our side. The idea is that if we pray, God will heal our land and we can go back to business as usual. That is not the way it works. That is not what Nehemiah did, nor what the rest of the scriptural passages say. When asked "Mr. President, do you think God is on our side?" Abraham Lincoln replied "Madame, the question is are we on God's side?" All of us personally must realize that we are saved by God's grace. We are still hopeless and helpless sinners. The rich young ruler couldn't work his way into heaven, and neither can we.

The third commonality is true repentance. God said in 2 Chronicles 7:14, "Turn from their wicked ways." Nehemiah wanted to do that by leading his people back to God. Jesus said in Matthew 6:9-14, "Forgive us our trespasses." As a nation, God is not likely to bless us if we simply pray and then go back to business as usual with no repentance and no remorse. Honest self-examination and true repentance for our acts should be considered an ongoing process.

The fourth commonality involves obedience. I believe obedience is strongly implied in the phrase in 2 Chronicles 7:14 "Seek my face." In other words, as Christ said in the Lord's Prayer, "Thy will be done." If we are not going to seek to understand and do God's will in our lives, as Nehemiah intended when he offered his prayer, I fail to see how God will truly bless our lives.

CONCLUSION

We have seen the commonalities of all scriptural prayer and the one difference between Old Testament prayer and New Testament prayer, that being the grace afforded us through Jesus. We have learned about how God wants us to approach prayer.

But we have one more lesson to learn from Nehemiah and his prayer. The remainder of the story of Nehemiah is recorded in Nehemiah's book. Nehemiah was not only appointed governor of Judea, but he was also given materials to do the work and safe passage back to Jerusalem. He was faced with a difficult task, enemies to face, and a recalcitrant people to work with. He succeeded anyway. He did this by restoring the worship of God and obedience to God's commandments. He also gave each family a portion of the wall to work on. Nehemiah said in his prayer that he, and his family, had sinned. The concept of the patriarch leading the family goes as far back in the scriptures, at least, to Joshua (Joshua 24:14–15), which states, "But as for me and my household, we will serve the Lord." So, Nehemiah challenged each family leader to lead their family. The task was accomplished in about two months using this method. In conclusion, the lesson is:

1. Pray first.
2. Gather your tools.
3. Lead your family.
4. Go out and get on the wall.

Discussion Questions

1. Baal was a "god of wood and stone" (Isaiah 37:19) created through the minds of men, that the pagans worshiped. While Baal is long gone, do we still worship "gods of wood and stone" in our society?
2. What does the term "Seek God's face", 2 Chronicles 7:14, mean, and how do we put that into action in our daily lives?

3. As a nation, how many examples can you cite showing that we have not "turned from our wicked ways" (2 Chronicles 7:14)?

4. The idea of repentance is a broad term. Discuss the full scope of repentance.

Chapter 4:

ON SOUND THEOLOGY
AND THE EMERGING
CHURCH IN AMERICA

"For the time will come when men will not put up with sound doctrine.
Instead, to suit their own desires, they will gather around them a great
number of teachers to say what their itching ears want to hear. They
will turn their heads away from the truth and turn aside to myths."
2 Timothy 4:3–4

INTRODUCTION

This is an analysis of and commentary on the philosophical and theological origins, current trends, doctrines, and
commonalities of a growing movement in America usually
referred to as the Emerging Church (EC). The emphasis will
be on discovering the commonalities of doctrine and examining their soundness and efficacy.

Emerging Church has been used in a very broad fashion, to
include mega-churches, denominationally affiliated churches
that simply do church differently, seeker-sensitive churches, and
nondenominational churches that vary widely in both doctrine
and practice. Painting with such a large brush inevitably leads
to gross mischaracterization of perfectly well-meaning groups

of people. To avoid that possibility, this essay will focus on doctrinal trends and commonalities within the movement, rather than serve as a general criticism. It should be noted that the term "emergent" church represents a very liberal movement led nominally by Brian McLaren and an organization called Emergent Village. The emergent church and McLaren's movement is not dealt with in this essay.

Although categories of ECs are quite blurred, all have some things in common. They are typically designed to reach unchurched people between the ages of 30–45, or from ages 35 on down, depending on the church. These are large groups in our society that traditional churches have failed to attract in large numbers. Many ECs do some things right. Many are theologically sound. From their efforts we may learn something valuable about both our way of doing things and about the younger people we are failing to reach. On the other side of the coin, some of the beliefs, doctrines, and practices of ECs run the gamut from downright heretical to just plain silly. Finally, we need to be both aware and fully informed of potentially dangerous shifts of doctrine in American Christianity because we have been warned many times in Scripture about false doctrines and false prophets (Matthew 24:24, Ephesians 4:14).[66]

A SYNOPSIS OF THE EMERGING CHURCH

First let's look at demographics, which I believe are the driving force behind ECs, mega-churches, and seeker-sensitive churches, all of which are completely co-mingled under the broad category of ECs. The ECs are specifically designed to attract groups

---

[66] Scott McKnight, "Five Streams of the Emerging Church", Christianity Today, February 2007, 35-39

of people who have no interest in, and are in fact largely repelled, by the more traditional church venues. This group contains a lot of people. The largest demographic group up until about 2000 was the baby boomers, now age fifty-five to seventy-five. Since the 1950s, this group has driven our economy, and hence our prosperity and ability to grow and spread the Gospel with our churches. Now, however, the largest demographic group that our nation has ever seen is the millennials, ages twenty-five to forty-one. At their peak, the baby boomers had eighty million people. Millennials have more than ninety million. They are now driving our economy. The problem is they are not driving the mission of many of our mainline denominations because, as a rule, they are notoriously reluctant to even attend a traditional church, much less join one.[67]

In 2014, two behavioral scientists did a survey and analysis of self-defined ECs called "The National Study of Youth and Religion."[68] The object of the survey was to discover the political views of ECs in relation to various mainline protestant denominations. The survey was conducted on individual churches identifying with ECs who were member churches of the various denominations surveyed. The survey found that, overall, seven percent of the mainline protestant churches identified themselves as an EC. The more liberal protestant denominations had a much higher percent of ECs than the more conservative denominations. Therefore, while the Disciples of Christ came in at almost fifteen percent and the United Methodists at ten percent, the Southern Baptists were

---

[67] US Census, 2010

[68] Christian Smith & Melinda Denton, The National Study of Youth and Religion, 2003, 1 wave, University of Notre Dame, 2003

only one percent EC.[69] Regardless, if one extrapolates these numbers, a rough approximation of EC membership nationwide might be around 3.5 million, not counting nondenominational churches.[70] This still leaves a very large untapped market among the 90 million millennials.

As a result, I believe, of this impending loss of largely untapped resources, both monetary and human, a movement began to attract the younger generations to church, starting quite early with Willow Creek Community Church, a nondenominational church in Chicago. Willow Creek is now a mega-church and is regarded as the business model for ambitious church planting in the post-modern era. It was started in 1975 by Bill Hybels, now retired. Many of the ideas adopted by Willow Creek also characterize many of the ECs. [71]

Those ideas and practices include a host of basic marketing concepts, all designed to remove all barriers to attendance. First, ECs adopt an agreeable name and attractive, modern logo. While this is anecdotal, it seems to me that ECs are almost always nonaffiliated and typically use the seeker-friendly word "community" in their name. The connotation here is that the people inside are a group of friends and neighbors just getting together for friendship, dialogue, and self-improvement. By way of contrast, my own church has the word "Baptist" on the sign in front and "Baptist" in the name. Sorry to say, this can repel the twenty- to forty-year-old group before they even give my church a chance to deliver the message.

---

[69] Ibid.

[70] Association of Religion Data Archives, www.thearda.com/archive

[71] Rich Tatum. "What Willow Creek's Reveal Study Really Tells Us". Tatumwebeb.com/blog/2008/06/05

Second, all rituals are eliminated, and services are informal, involving state-of-the-art multimedia technology, contemporary, popular Christian music, lots of electric instruments, informal attire, and a very short message involving a narrative or dialogue. Other techniques are used in the service to avoid the appearance of acting judgmental or dictatorial in any way. One pastor of a nondenominational mega church wears blue jeans and no necktie to preach on Sundays. He is also quite proud of the fact that he infrequently quotes the scriptures.[72]

Third, there is a host of conveniences designed to make church-going hassle-free, including day-care for every function, movie night, various activities, and small group study (typically referred to in conventional churches as Sunday school). Anecdotally, I am told Willow Creek has a Starbucks and a McDonald's in the lobby of the church building, which I am also told looks like a mall.

Finally, the ECs are very service oriented, expecting all members to serve in some capacity. The ECs are known for being heavily involved in community service projects of one sort or another. It may be said that ECs are generally missional in their focus on doing something good in the current culture, particularly in regard to the poor. ECs try to find a purpose for everyone.[73]

While many evangelical churches, including my own, incorporate many or most of the above practices and techniques, the core difference between conservative evangelical churches, Southern Baptists, and the ECs lies squarely in doctrinal beliefs: what people are taught about our religion, how they are fed by

---

[72] Gabe Hughes. "These Words Shall Be on your Heart". Junction City 1 Southern Baptist Church, pastorgabehughes.Blogspot.com 9/12/2016

[73] Paul Enns. The Moody Handbook of Theology. Chicago: Moody Press, 1986, 1994

the church, and how they mature as Christians. We will take a close, hard look at the doctrinal trends in the ECs in a critical fashion, to see whether the effort to attract our young people to become involved is truly a positive mission to do God's work, or a manifestation of false doctrine.

Regarding a belief system, as all sources indicate, there really isn't a formalized type of belief system, as would be the case for a formal denomination.[74] Even if aligned with a denomination, I suspect that a *de facto* EC would be on the fringes of the official doctrine. The reason this may be so is that, typically, ECs don't like formal doctrine, having rejected what Dr. Dean, in her book, *Almost Christian*,[75] calls the "authoritative community." This abandonment of rigid doctrinal statements is yet another effort on the part of the EC community to attempt to be relevant to the post-modern culture going on around us. As the pastor for a neighborhood branch of a traditional United Methodist church said, "We're trying to become a much more diverse church and contextualize to the neighborhood we find ourselves in," and "[we are] focused on bridging divides in the community."[76] A hallmark of the ECs is the desire to appear tolerant, inclusive, non-offensive and "[with] emphasis on developing relationships with non-believers."[77]

This missional type of practice, and desire to appear tolerant and inclusive has led to what is apparently a quite common belief in universalism. Universalism can be defined, according

---

[74] Ibid.

[75] Kenda Creasy Dean. Almost Christian. New York: Oxford University Press, 2010

[76] Madison Iszler. "NC Churches Reach Out To a Younger Crowd", Jefferson City News Tribune, 11/6/2016

[77] Hughes, Ibid.

to Paul Enns,[78] as the denial of the concept of hell and final judgment. This can be extended to the belief that all religions are basically the same, worshiping the same god under a different name, based on the culture the religion has appeared in, and usually referred to as a "tradition." Universalism seems to hold that there is a generic god, a "Mcgod," who really doesn't care which tradition you practice, so long as you are a nice person and are nice to other people. The logic is that God will provide for everyone to eventually go to heaven. The study Dr. Dean wrote about in *Almost Christian* [79] found this belief to appear more frequently than any other concept among young people. Universalism also includes a belief commonly held by people I consider the leading edge of the EC movement, those being Rob Bell, Brian McLaren, Tony Jones, and Doug Pagitt among others, who hold that there is no hell, and no need for hell, because eventually everyone will be redeemed by God. Therefore, God really doesn't intend to judge anyone, and eschatology is almost totally avoided in the EC churches, preferring the doctrine of: It will all work out OK in the end, whatever that end is, if there is any end at all. This leads me to my next point.

The EC churches have made a concerted effort to deconstruct the Bible partially or completely, reducing the Scriptures to narratives designed to tell a simple, clearly understandable and thoroughly agreeable Bible story. These narratives are designed to make people feel good about themselves (at this point, the phrase "warm and fuzzy" is frequently used by detractors). Deconstruction is a long-time benchmark of liberal theology (more on this later). At its extreme, and some of the ECs are extreme, virtually nothing in the Bible that may be

---

[78] Enns, Ibid.

[79] Dean, Ibid.

confusing, seemingly unrelated to current society, violent, or in any way disturbing, is taken at face value. Also, nothing is taken at face value that could possibly contradict the personal value systems of the EC or its members. Liberalism in theology, as Paul Enns states, "Places a premium on man's reason and the findings of science; whatever does not agree with reason and science is to be rejected."[80]

The hallmark of liberal theologians was, and is, the allegorical method of interpreting the Bible. Dwight Pentecost, in his benchmark work *Things to Come*,[81] defines the allegorical method as "the method of interpreting a literary text that regards the literal sense as the vehicle for a secondary, more spiritual and more profound sense. ...The historical import is either denied or ignored and the emphasis is placed entirely on a secondary sense so that the original words or events have little or no significance.... It would seem that the purpose of the allegorical method is not to interpret scripture, but to pervert the true meaning of scripture, albeit under the guise of seeking a deeper or more spiritual meaning."

What I believe will become an instant classic of the liberal, deconstructionist genre is a 2014 book, *The Bible Tells Me So...* by Peter Enns (no relation to Paul Enns, the author of the textbook) who holds a PhD from Harvard. Here are some samples from Peter Enns' book *The Bible Tells Me So...*[82] "Jesus, like other Jews of the first century, read His Bible creatively, seeking deeper meaning that transcended or simply bypassed the boundaries of the words of scripture," and "the biblical writers were storytellers. Writing about the past was never simply about understanding

---

[80] Enns, Ibid. 593

[81] J. Dwight Pentecost. Things to Come. Grand Rapids: Zondervan, 1958, page 4

[82] Peter Enns. "The Bible Tells Me So". New York: HarperCollins, 2014

the past for its own sake, but about shaping, molding, and creating the past to speak to the present. Getting the past right wasn't the driving issue. "Who we are now" was the important matter. (Note: Remember, Peter Enns is referring to the Son of God and the people who wrote the Bible here. He apparently thinks they made it up.) The liberal theology of deconstruction and allegory, as demonstrated above, has had, in my opinion, a profound effect on our churches, particularly mainline protestant churches since World War II, and constitutes an important, if informal, doctrinal foundation of the ECs as they attempt to be inclusive, tolerant, and inoffensive.

Other commonalities in the ECs include the necessity for the message and the ministry of the church to be relevant to the current culture, including the significant political issues of the time. The Burge/Djupe[83] study identifies the four most important political issues for the ECs currently as same-sex marriage, the environment, abortion, and foreign policy. Relevancy extends to personal and community issues as well and the ECs are typically service-oriented, particularly in service to the poor and other alternative communities.

In my opinion, the most disturbing trend in the EC belief system is a marked tendency to embrace relativism in message, doctrine, and practice. Relativism is founded on the belief that there are no objective absolutes, no objective truth, and no objective standards with which to judge right and wrong or good and evil. In doctrinal terms, this inevitably leads to a belief system in which the Scriptures are not only not inerrant but simply wrong in various respects. As stated above,

---

[83] Ryan P. Burge and Paul A. Djupe. "Truly Inclusive or Uniformly Liberal? An Analysis of the Politics of the Emerging Church". Journal for the Scientific Study of Religion, 53, no.3, (September 2014) 636-651

deconstruction of the Bible, universalism, and some truly creative allegorical interpretations are the result. In short, a relativistic worldview allows the tolerance or acceptance of almost anything and the subjective rewriting and interpretation of the Scriptures for oneself. This includes the idea that what is right for me may be wrong for you and that my truth is as valid as anyone else's because it is based on my experiential knowledge.

Included in the relativistic worldview, another hallmark of the ECs, is the belief that church should be relational, regarding everyone's "life story" as being valid and acceptable. ECs are much more concerned with relating to everyone's feelings than feeding their minds with knowledge.

All of this leads to a final, overarching commonality among ECs, that commonality being the totally self-absorbed nature of the above-described church belief system. Practically everything surrounding an EC is "all about me." EC members get to decide whether the Bible is right for them, whether their lifestyle is OK, whether they are a nice enough people to go to heaven, and what parts of God's plan they like and are therefore going to accept and what parts they don't like and aren't going to accept. This is all about feelings rather than thought. How one feels about the various matters of doctrine and practice is the most important concept in the ECs.

The basic belief system, then, particularly of the younger people in, or out of, the ECs is perfectly characterized by Aaron Rodgers, long-time quarterback for the Green Bay Packers and likely Hall-of-Famer. When asked about his religious views in an interview, Rodgers stated, "Ultimately it was the rules and regulations and binary systems that really don't resonate with me.... I don't know how you can believe in a God who wants to condemn most of the planet to a fiery hell. What type of loving, sensitive, omnipresent, omnipotent being wants to condemn his beautiful creation to a fiery hell at the end of all of this?" Here Rodgers demonstrates perfectly the belief system I am afraid is all too common in our society, particularly in our younger people. The result, then, seems to me to be a completely self-absorbed doctrine designed to simply fill the pews and coffers on a Sunday morning. Otherwise, it is theologically, biblically, and spiritually bankrupt.

ORIGINS

> "The past isn't dead – it isn't even past
> -William Faulkner -

At this point it would be instructive to put the concepts and doctrines of the ECs in context, to learn where they came from and how we got to this point. Two movements, which began before the turn of the twentieth century, have heavily influenced thought up to the present, including theological thought. Those political, economic, social, and religious movements are Marxist socialism and Ideological Darwinism. Toward the beginning of the twentieth century, those two movements made something of a syncretistic combination, which eventually resulted in secular humanism and the extreme liberal, or post-modern, theology now seen in some EC churches.

First, Ideological Darwinism. Charles Darwin, (1809–1882), turned out to be a most important passenger on the exploratory voyage of the HMS Beagle in 1831. Darwin, an upper-class Englishman with an interest in the natural sciences, published his findings as the result of that voyage in 1857. In *On the Origin of Species,* Darwin called his hypothesis the "theory of evolution." Darwin's hypothesis was that every species, including man, had evolved from something else through the process of natural adaptation. In natural adaptation, species, to survive, adapt to their surroundings. This is also called survival of the fittest. Doing this for long periods of time results in the evolution of the original species, becoming an entirely new species. Darwin hypothesized that man had evolved from the lower apes, becoming smarter, walking upright, and becoming able to think logically as the result of a long process of adaptation.

In England, Darwin's theory was popular, if not scientifically proven. It was so popular, in fact, it began to be applied not only to science but to economics, social theory, government, and religion. Ideological Darwin supporters reasoned that, if man had evolved on his own, then not only was there no need for God but there was no need for a creator at all. The creationists and the evolutionist met at the local schoolhouse, when the government decided to teach the new theory in science class, hence the Scopes monkey trial.

Slightly later, Karl Marx (1818–1883), a German immigrant also living in England, published his first volume of a three-volume economic treatise called Das Kapital (1857). In it, Marx framed the concepts of what we now call socialism, both as an economic theory and as a social theory. Marx maintained that religion was simply a tool used by the wealthy controlling elite to keep the working class both ignorant and compliant. In Das Kapital, he stated, "Man makes religion, religion does not make man." He went on to say that religion was an invention of the state and "The sigh of the oppressed creature, the heart of a heartless world, and the soul of soulless conditions. It is the opium of the people." Marx was presumably an atheist. He believed in a statist solution to everything, including the application of the means of production, government provision of living standards, and the confiscation and redistribution of wealth. In the Marxian system, there was no room for religion.

The government was the supreme problem-solver and arbiter of social conduct and belief.

Marx's ideas became popular, particularly with the populists, labor unions, and social reformers of the turn of the twentieth century in America. A syncretistic belief system emerged from a combination of the two ideologies, called secular humanism, which has had a profound effect on the theology of the twentieth and twenty-first centuries and has manifested itself in the doctrines of the ECs.

Secular humanism, now called post-modernism, incorporates the ideas of both Marx and Darwin. Like the Darwinian ideologues, modern secular humanists believe that man has evolved from the lower forms, as have all creatures and all life on the planet. This is called the "cosmic accident" theory. This has given rise to the thought that man can place himself in the position of God and create a society that is good and just. The only moral authority in society is the government. Secular humanists favor the social justice causes, as does the EC, and believe it is our government's duty to provide and enforce laws promoting social justice and redistribution of wealth. Secular humanists believe in a government of men, not of laws. In the world of the secular humanist, there are no absolutes, including the Scriptures. Everything is relative, experiential, and subjective. Finally, most secular humanists believe, as Marx did, that man creates God, God doesn't create man. Erasing all mention or memory of the Christian religion from the public marketplace of ideas, as we have seen in America for some time, is a secular humanist goal. Some of the dirty laundry of secular humanism includes the concept of eugenics, pioneered by Margaret Sanger, and used to terrible effect by the Nazis, and the theories of public education of John Dewey, inspired by ideological Darwinism. [84]

ANALYSIS AND CONCLUSIONS

The ideology of secular humanism has produced a belief system that is founded on the erudition of man. Any belief system which is founded on the erudition of man requires far too much faith and contains far too little objective truth. Secular humanism is an ideology based on man reaching up to become God, rather than God reaching down to redeem man. The ECs have, to some degree, fallen victim to this false doctrine.

The most startling examples I found to illustrate this point appear in Peter Enns' (no relation to Paul Enns) book T*he Bible Tells Me So*, cited above. As Peter Enns' sarcastic title would suggest, Enns basically formed his own translation of Scripture. A brief summary of Enns' points include, the Jews made up the part about God ordering them to kill every living thing in Deuteronomy 20:18 and Joshua 10:40 to cover up an atrocity. Jesus distorted the Old Testament to fit the message that He was Messiah. The Apostles distorted the Gospels to fit the Messiah narrative. There is no mention in Enns' book of the Revelation (the ECs don't talk about judgment). I might note that Enns' book is highly endorsed by Rob Bell, Brian McLaren, and Tony Jones, all of whom I referred to earlier as the leading edge of the EC movement.

When I began my research for this chapter, I was fairly neutral in regard to the EC movement. After all, it is hard to argue with a movement that puts tens of thousands of people in the

---

[84] David A. Noebel. Understanding The Times. Eugene: Harvest House Publishers, 1991

pews every Sunday morning. But the more I researched the movement, the more charlatans and false doctrine I found. The completely secular humanist "theology" of Peter Enns is just one example.

This very liberal and secular humanist interpretation of the scriptures, which has worked its way into many churches and doctrines, both Protestant and Catholic, is the result of the above-described ideologies, but also the result of the phenomenon of higher level academic criticism. And, while Peter Enns is perfectly free to write whatever he wants, Jesus has something to say about it.

In Matthew 12:30 Jesus states, "He that is not with me is against me; and he that gathereth not with me scattereth abroad." And again, more telling, in Matthew 24:24, "For there shall arise false Christs, and false prophets, and shall show great signs and wonders." Finally, the most telling of all, Matthew 7:19–23 states, "Not everyone who says to me 'Lord, Lord' will enter the kingdom of heaven, but only he who does the will of my father who is in heaven. Many will say to me in that day, 'Lord, Lord, have we not prophesied in thy name? And in thy name have cast out devils? And in thy name done many wonderful works?' And then I will profess unto them, I never knew you. Depart from me, ye that work iniquity."

This becomes dramatically and sadly apparent in Dr. Deans review of the National Study of Youth and Religion in her book *Almost Christian*. The teenagers surveyed in that book, which was published in 2010, are now the target market for the EC movement. The study found that their theology consists of the following: I'm a nice person. God wants people to be good, nice, and fair to each other, and all world religions share this view. God is not involved in our everyday lives and I only seek God to solve a problem. Good people (of all religions) go to heaven when they die. I'm a good person.[85]As was pointed out in Matthew 12:30, God does not give out participation trophies. You either win or you lose.

To call this weak theology would be paying it a compliment. The first phrase that came to mind was "immature Christianity", much as Paul talks about in Ephesians 4:11–14. Dr. Dean and the people who did the study call it "Moralistic Therapeutic Deism." I could not think of a more descriptive and more accurate term. In a very blunt passage in Revelation 3:15–18, Jesus gives us clear warning by saying:

> "I know your deeds, that you are neither cold nor hot.
> I wish you were either one or the other! So, because
> you are luke-warm - neither hot nor cold - I am
> about to spit you out of my mouth. You say, "I am
> rich; I have acquired wealth and do not need a thing"
> But you do not realize that you are wretched, pitiful,
> poor, blind, and naked. I counsel you to buy gold
> refined in the fire, so you can become rich."

Considering the above, I believe we have a call to stand firm in our churches and families in upholding the integrity and truth of the scriptures. This cannot be the age of compromise, convenience, and comfort simply to get people to become associated with a church of one sort or another. A large portion of our youth depend on us to pass down a strong and mature faith. The Apostle Paul sums this up in Ephesians 4:14–15, which states, "Then we will no longer be infants, tossed back and forth by the waves, and blown here and there by every wind of doctrine and by the cunning and craftiness of men in their

---

[85] Dean, Ibid., page 14 et. Seq.

deceitful scheming. Instead, speaking the truth in love, we will in all things grow up into him who is head, that is, Christ."

DISCUSSION QUESTIONS

1. What important theological concepts from the Bible are rarely, if ever, discussed in an EC?
2. How would you respond to Aaron Rodgers?
3. Dr. Kenda Dean, in her book *Almost Christian*, points out that the current trend in liberal theology began in earnest following World War II. What institutions, groups, or people do you believe failed the generations now under 40 years old?
4. What would you suggest Christians do to reclaim their young people?

Chapter 5:
ON DEFENSE OF THE FAITH

(An Apologetic)
"Human history is the long terrible story of man trying to find something other than God which will make him happy."
C.S. Lewis

THE PURPOSE OF APOLOGETICS

> "My purpose is that they may be encouraged in heart...
> so that they may have the full riches of complete
> understanding, in order that they may know the
> mystery of God...
>
> Apostle Paul, Colossians 2:2

INTRODUCTION

Practically everyone has a worldview. It may be one that relies on false notions. It may not be well thought out. And it may be as simple as the one attributed to the late Jackie Gleason, who said, "He who dies with the most toys, wins." But we all have a worldview that we have formed in an attempt to understand the point and purpose of our lives, our surroundings, and our universe in general.

Douglas Groothuis explained worldview as being our concepts and answers regarding ultimate reality. This includes "The complex of concepts that explains and gives meaning to reality from where [we] stand."[86] Those complex concepts that make up our worldview might include our views of history, biological science, behavioral science, economics, political science, work, family, and a host of other considerations both great and small. To a great extent, our worldview rests on the foundations of our religious beliefs or lack of them. Our worldview is defined by our view of religion—whatever that may be. This has been true for all people across both time and cultural boundaries.[87]

Apologetics is the discipline of explaining in a rational, logical, and convincing fashion, the objective truth of our worldview in the context of a belief system. Groothuis states, "A hearty, sturdy, and insatiable appetite for reality—whatever it might be—is the only engine for testing and discerning the truth." Knowing the objective truth should be the goal of Christian apologetics.[88]

Particularly, during this time in the history of our nation and the Church, everyone in the pews needs to be strong and fully informed in the concepts and truisms of our beliefs. Faith is fine, and necessary for all Christians at some point, but now we urgently need the systematic concepts, knowledge, and answers embodied in the study of apologetics to face and overcome widespread and growing apostasy and hostility, particularly in our own society. Whether we know it or not, we are at

---

[86] Douglas Groothuis, *Christian Apologetics: A Comprehensive Case for Biblical Faith*, (Downers Grove: InterVarsity Press, USA, 2011)

[87] Samuel P. Huntington, *The Clash of Civilizations*, (New York: Simon and Schuster Paperbacks, 1996) 42

[88] James K. Beilby, Thinking About Christian Apologetics, (Downers Grove: InterVarsity Press, USA, 2011) Ibid., 28

war (Eph. 6:12). Christianity in America, and particularly evangelical Christianity, has stirred up both positive and negative discussion by our politicians and media, some who know what they are talking about and some who don't.

Illustrative of the state of Christianity among many people, and particularly our younger people, is a statement made by Aaron Rodgers several years ago in a live interview. For those of you who are not football fans, Aaron Rodgers is 38 years old, a millennial, and long-time quarterback of the Green Bay Packers. Rodgers has one Super Bowl ring and is a likely Hall-of-Famer. When asked about his religious beliefs, Rodgers replied, "Ultimately, it was the rules and regulations and binary systems [that] don't resonate with me. [This] led down a different path of spirituality — I don't know how you can believe in a God who wants to condemn most of the planet to a fiery hell. What type of loving, sensitive, omnipresent, omnipotent being wants to condemn his beautiful creation to a fiery hell at the end of all of this?"

This is emblematic of and quite typical of many Americans, and particularly people under age forty. At base, Rodgers' statement is one all of us need to be able to respond to.

Modern Philosophy

This section consists of an examination and comparison of the worldviews of Secular Humanism (hereinafter Humanism), and Christianity, particularly evangelical Christianity, to compare the two very disparate belief systems and make an objective determination of the truth of each. The fundamental, keystone beliefs of each worldview, those beliefs and assumptions which support the whole of the belief system, will be detailed, and analyzed to make this determination.

In regard to Humanism, it must first be noted that I use the term "Humanism" to include a host of philosophies spanning both the nineteenth and twentieth centuries. Along with Secular Humanism, these include:

- **Marxist Socialism:** An agnostic ideology in which the State is the only governing entity and in which the people serve only the State. The Church is, therefore, the enemy.
- **Materialism:** A belief in what physically exists and can be seen in the universe.
- **Rationalism:** A complete belief only in science and what can physically be proven. Both materialism and rationalism, to one degree or another, do not believe in the existence of a spiritual realm, predictive prophecy, or miracles.
- **Post-Modernism:** Commonly thought to be the philosophy of the twenty-first century, combines the elements from all the above belief systems.

The fundamentals of Secular Humanism, together with the various philosophies above are:

1. Most Humanists are either atheist or agnostic. They embrace the concepts of scientific naturalism, this is to say they do not acknowledge any supernatural occurrences whatsoever, including creation, miracles, the resurrection, the existence of a soul, or life after death. Humanists believe the Earth came into existence, and subsequently into its present form, as the result of happenstance and is self-existing. Humanists rely strictly on scientific knowledge to reveal the truth of this assertion.

2. Evolution. Humanists adhere to the theories of evolution. There are several current variations on the theory of evolution, including process theology. As science progresses these various theories regarding the mechanisms of evolution have changed.
3. Ethics, therefore, are regarded as "consequentialist" in nature i.e., judged by their results. This is usually referred to as "the ends justify the means."
4. Humanism, therefore, is uniquely focused on man and man's ability, typically achieved through "observation, experimentation, and rational analysis," to achieve "man's highest ideals."[89]

The contrasting fundamentals of Christianity are:

1. God exists and has always existed, in triune form. He revealed through Scriptures that He created the Earth out of nothing. There are scientific, mathematical, and rational grounds for this assertion.
2. God then created all living things.
3. As His final creative act, God created man as a special creature, able to think, reason, and recognize the God that created him.
4. The Scriptures make up the fundamental basis of the Christian worldview, specifically telling modern man that numbers one and two are true. The historical accuracy and reliability of the Bible can be shown. Ethics, therefore, are not optional and up to each individual

[89] Tom Flynn, *Secular Humanism Defined*, (Council for Secular Humanism, , 11/22/2017)

but specified throughout God's Word. The ends *do not* justify the means.

5. Both the Bible and historic experience informs that man cannot, on his own, attain the highest ideals nor can he successfully govern himself. This is the result of sin, defined as acting outside the will of God. The Bible also tells us, in Revelation, God's plan for His creation when man reaches the point where man almost winds up causing his own destruction. God drives history.[90]

THE HUMANIST WORLDVIEW

Humanists, generally, don't acknowledge the existence of God or, if they do, they do not believe in a God who is active and concerned about the lives of men. As a result, Humanism embraces the concept of scientific naturalism, which holds that everything in the universe operates as a closed system and should be investigated purely on natural terms, through science. Humanists deny any supernatural events based on the idea that they are scientifically impossible, un-provable, or mere superstition. Therefore, as the creation was a supernatural event and can't, at least for the Humanists, be proven through hard science, there was no creation event and God doesn't exist. The scriptural account is regarded as a so-called "creation myth." The ultimate authority, therefore, is man himself, alone in the universe. Since there was no creation event, the existence of the natural world, all living things, and man, simply evolved from what is generally referred to as "primordial soup." This theory is regarded as settled science by many Humanists, Naturalists,

---

[90] Douglas Groothuis, *Christian Apologetics: A Comprehensive Case for Biblical Faith*, (Downer's Grove: InterVarsityPress, USA, 2011)

and others. The Humanist societies insist that it be taught in all public schools and occasionally object when evolution is referred to as a theory, not a fact.[91]

While the thought and philosophy behind Humanism began during the eighteenth century Enlightenment, when Charles Darwin published his findings, in 1859 in *On the Origin of Species*, Humanism became popularized. Darwin proposed the theory of evolution as an extension of the idea of natural adaptation of species to allow the species to survive in the environment. Darwin's theory caught on rapidly, not as good science, but as an ideological concept. Among other things, at the turn of the twentieth century this resulted in a liberal theological assault through form, source, and literary criticism of the Bible. The popularity of Humanism as a belief system crystalized the Humanist worldview and the adoption of both Darwinism and scientific naturalism as the standards of the movement.[92]

Recently, the idea of process theology has been added as a modern scientific support for the general concept of evolution. As originally proposed by Darwin, the forming of new species occurred gradually, with multiple adaptations eventually changing DNA and the species itself. Later, when the fossil record and scientific advancement failed to support gradual evolution, it was theorized that evolution between species occurred rapidly as the result of gene mutation caused by isolation. Finally, with process theology, which is a complex theory involving intercellular material and which is the province of bio-geneticists, the subatomic particles in each cell, through constant activity and generation of energy, introduce molecular

---

[91] Tom Flynn, *Secular Humanism Defined*, *(Council* for Secular Humanism, , 11/22/2017)

[92] Tim LaHaye, and David A. Noebel, *Mind Siege*, (Nashville: Thomas Nelson, 2000)

changes in DNA. This transformation causes species to evolve. Regardless of the mechanics, Humanists believe that species, including man, evolved from the primordial soup and are still evolving. Man will eventually evolve into a higher, better, smarter species, capable of solving all of man's current problems. This is the realistic theory of knowledge for the humanist.[93]

The source of morality for the Humanist is contained in various man-made manifestos and seems to be fairly universally agreed upon. The manifestos are centered on man himself and man acting corporately in ways that lead to happiness for humans. For example, "Secular humanists hold that ethics is consequential, to be judged by the results. Secular humanists seek to develop and improve their ethical principles by examining the results they yield in the lives of real men and women" and "the lifestance of Humanism—guided by reason, inspired by compassion, and informed by experience—encourages us to live life well and fully. It evolved through the ages and continues to develop through the efforts of thoughtful people who recognize that values and ideals, however carefully wrought, are subject to change as our knowledge and understandings advance." Morality, ethics, and the concept of right and wrong seem to all be relative and changeable, depending on the needs and demands of society.[94]

Finally, in terms of human impact in the real world, while not exclusively Humanist, the Humanist worldview has typically embraced social justice issues and socialist economic concepts of one variety or another. The Humanists rely on government for two important things. The first is that Humanists

---

[93] L. Russ Bush, *The Advancement*, (Nashville: B&H Academic, 2003)

[94] Humanist Manifestos I – 1933, II – 1973, and III – Humanism and its Aspirations, 2003

insist on a complete and total separation of church and state, to include the elimination of any reference to religion in the public sector. The second is that Humanists insist on evolution in the science curriculum of the public schools to the exclusion of all theories involving creationism. Humanists also favor taxpayer funded abortion on demand, redistribution of wealth based on fairness and compassion, and various other social justice issues. Generally, Humanists believe in the concept of universalism, which is the idea that all societies, cultures, and nations are equally rational and basically good. Therefore, ideally, all mankind should, and will eventually, evolve into a single society of peace and happiness.[95]

Most Humanists hold to a belief system starting from the position of atheism and running to a mild form of deism or agnosticism, which tends toward the semi-Buddhist (or Hindu) concept of a universal spiritual oneness. This belief may include spirits in inanimate objects and animals, called animism. Typically, the Humanist writers and philosophers simply express the atheist position. Humanists strictly disavow any supernatural events, or miracles, because all events must have a scientific explanation. Therefore, Humanists have adopted a position of scientific naturalism, which holds that Earth arose spontaneously, as the result of sequential cosmic accidents, and that those fortuitous natural events eventually led to the formation of the planet and everything on it. These events were, and continue to be, naturally occurring scientific phenomena, happening as a matter of random chance.[96]

---

[95] Ibid.

[96] Ibid.

CRITICISM

First, the logic behind the atheist position is not well grounded in positive proof and fact. It begins with the scientific ideas from Charles Darwin and his theory of evolution. The logic seems to be that, if Darwin is correct and all life on Earth evolved, slowly or suddenly, as the result of various biological and environmental conditions, then there was no supernatural creation at all and Earth and everything on it is a chance event. If there was no supernatural creation event, then there is no need for a creator. Therefore, there are only two forces— nature and man—at work on the planet. The Humanists, then, actually work backwards in an attempt to disprove an already well-founded and widely held belief that God exists.[97]

The Humanist belief system is not factually adequate, particularly since it results in such a profound conclusion of atheism. Some scientists seem utterly convinced that evolution is a proven fact and that the Earth was not formed by a creator. However mathematics—particularly the field of probability and statistics—does not support the "cosmic accident" conclusion. The cosmic events that necessarily took place to form the Earth, which we barely understand now, are highly unlikely to have happened at the right time, in the right place, and with the right outcomes to produce the conditions necessary for life on Earth. These events had to have happened in exactly the right sequence for the correct outcome.[98]

Mathematically, the probability of each separate event must be multiplied (X) by the next event to produce a result. For example, event No. 1. There is a sun conducive to life on Earth,

---

[97] Groothuis, Ibid.

[98] Bush, Ibid.

(X) No. 2. With appropriate gravity (X) No. 3. Also, with appropriate light (X) No. 4. Located in a relatively quiet region of the galaxy (X) No. 5. With an iron-core planet in perfect orbit, or "Goldilocks Zone," (X) No. 6. With sufficient water for life (X) No. 7. With a viable atmosphere (X) No. 8. Rotating at a specific angle (X) No. 9. With sufficient land mass to accommodate life and oxygen exchange (X) No. 10. With carbon, to support carbon-based life forms. This formula goes on all the way up to the probability of the evolution of man. The probability calculation, if extended all the way to the likelihood of a chance infusion of energy, perhaps by a lightning bolt striking just the right place in the primordial soup, to infuse enough energy to create DNA, (even in the simplest life forms DNA is marvelously complex) and therefore begin life, shows a likelihood that life occurred spontaneously on Earth as a one in ten chance to an unimaginable power in the billions, making the cosmic accident virtually impossible.

The Christian version of creation is written in the first chapter of Genesis, featuring God, called *Elohim,* meaning "Creator." God created the universe from nothing. Humanists regard this passage as a complete myth. But again, sequence of events is important here. It seems that the Genesis account breaks creation down into six separate acts. Each of the acts depict a step in the creation process. Recently, science also has formed a theory as to how our planet came to be in the form it is now and what the sequence of those events were. The sequence of events proposed by science is roughly the same as the sequence of events depicted in the creation account in the first chapter of Genesis, which was written by Moses in 1450 BC. The ancient Hebrews could not possibly have known anything about how the planet was formed, what was on it, or how it worked. In fact, they had nowhere near the scientific knowledge necessary to form our current theory regarding the formation of Earth. Logic leads one to the conclusion: The creation story is true, accurate, and that Moses was inspired by God to write it down.

Finally, there is a serious question regarding the Big Bang theory. If there is no God, then, presumably, the universe itself was spontaneously created. Current scientific theory indicates that this occurred when a very small but extremely dense piece of matter, containing enough energy to power the universe, exploded. This explosion caused a chain reaction, leading to the formation of stars, planets, and galaxies. While the theory itself is credible, and God could have started the universe that way, one question remains. Where did the original piece of matter come from? If the Big Bang is correct, according to naturalism, the universe spontaneously occurred from that first tiny piece of matter. But no one has any idea where that first matter came from. Nature cannot make something out of nothing, but the Bible tells us that God did just that.

The next step in the Humanist philosophy is the concept of Darwinism itself, also known as the theory of evolution. Over the years, humanists have had increasing difficulty logically and rationally explaining the nuts and bolts of evolution, partly as the result of scientific advancement in the fields of anthropology, genetics, mathematics, and molecular biology. Recently a change has occurred, an ad hoc readjustment in the theory of evolution. This change is the result of advances in molecular biology, as set out in L. Russ Bush's book, *The Advancement*. This has given rise to the theory of Process Theology. It is called that because of the process that takes place with subatomic material inside atoms, which is thought to be the driving force for life and evolution. Darwin and his contemporaries thought that evolution occurred slowly and as the result of numerous adaptations for survival. Eventually, they believed a new species would emerge. The fossil record failed to bear this out, so it was proposed that evolution occurred through rapid mutation, typically brought about by the isolation of a species. This too cannot be proven, even in controlled conditions. Finally, as the result of the development of microbiology, the study of sub-atomic matter has given rise to the theory that constant energy provoking change in subatomic particles is what causes DNA to change and the species to evolve. This phenomenon cannot be shown in a lab either. So, the first criticism of the naturalist, evolutionist belief system is that it is neither factually adequate nor realistic.[99]

It can also be pointed out that our own species, homo sapiens, has not changed since the earliest evidence of modern man some 250,000 to 300,000 years ago. A Humanist conten-tion is that man will evolve into a better, smarter, more suc-cessful species. However, no evidence exists that this has taken place or that it even *can* take place.

As a final insult to evolutionary theories, there are the rather recent scientific developments involving the Cretaceous-Paleogene (K-Pg) boundary. The K-Pg boundary is a thin layer of ash and other minerals lying between strata from the Cretaceous and Paleogene Periods and dates back approxi-mately 56 million years ago. (Until recently this was called the K-T boundary, and the T stood for Tertiary.) Through the work of Eugene Shoemaker (1928–1997) and others, it was deter-mined that a meteor struck Earth some 56 million years ago in the Gulf of Mexico off the Yucatan Peninsula. It caused such environmental havoc that all the dinosaurs were wiped out. To date, no dinosaur fossils have ever been found above the K-Pg boundary. Scientists believe that the only surviving life on Earth

---

[99] Bush, Ibid.

after the meteor strike were some fish, a few birds, and small rodents. Given any of the mechanisms proposed for evolution, it is difficult to imagine a scenario in which the DNA code of these remaining species changed and evolved to such an extent and magnitude as to become the large diversity of species we have today, including man. DNA is complex. Mathematically, the probability of multiple DNA changes in species occurring by random chance, even over a period of fifty million years or more, is virtually zero. Darwinian evolution, while easy to conceptualize for most people, is very thin stuff on which to base a worldview in terms of facts, reality, and viability.[100]

The Humanist source of morality is the Humanists themselves. There are some general principles, vague at best, that seem to form this moral code. In the end, however, Humanist ethics seem to begin and end with socialist public policy, such as redistribution of the wealth to those less fortunate and taxpayer funded abortion on demand. Humanists are moral relativists. All things change and concepts of morals, ethics, right and wrong, and even good and evil, should change to meet the needs and demands of society. The humanists never specify as to who will decide what the standards for society are going to be or when they will change, just that they will be decided by men in some agreed-upon fashion. The Humanist position also seems to incorporate John Stuart Mill's theory of utilitarian ethics, which states, "The right thing to do is the one that produces the most good for the greatest number of people." As a practical matter, all this boils down to one of the fundamentals of moral relativism, and that is "the ends justify the means."[101]

---

[100] LaHaye, Ibid.

[101] A Secular Humanist Declaration, (Council for Democratic and Secular Humanism, , 11/22/2017)

The Christian Worldview

A Christian, by definition, is a person who has accepted Jesus Christ as the Son of God and personal savior. Christians not only believe that God exists, but also that He is the Creator of the Universe. As part of that creation, God made man "in our image, to be like us" (Gen. 1:26, NLT). Man is special, a sentient being capable of creative, imaginative, and original thought, and unlike anything else in God's creation. Man can identify and understand God, to the extent that is possible. The God of the Christians is one, meaning that He is a specific God and the *only* God. He is identified as the God of Abraham, Isaac, and Jacob. He is the God who chose the Jews to be His people. In Scripture, God is identified first as *Elohim*, or "Creator," and later as Jehovah, the only actual proper name for God, and meaning the unchanging, eternal, and self-existing God, expressed as "I am that I am" to Moses in Exodus 3:14. The Christian God is a God of justice and grace who loves His creation corporately and individually. The Bible makes it clear that God is manifest in three forms, the Father, the Son (Jesus Christ) and the Holy Spirit. This is known as the triune God. Jesus, then, was both fully God and fully human, on Earth as a real person. [102]

For a Christian, the proof of both God's existence and God's identity is found in The Holy Bible. The Bible itself is the foundation of faith. Christians embrace the belief system of the Bible. The Bible is made up of sixty-six separate books written by about forty men over a period of approximately 1,500 years. Not counting the creation and the flood, the events in the Bible span the period of time from Abraham (2165 BC) to

---

[102] Thomas D. Lea and David Alan Black, The New Testament: Its Background and its Message, Second Edition, (Nashville: B&H Academic, 2003)

first century Palestine, which is a remarkable 2,265-year period. The forty plus authors of the books of the Bible were inspired by God in their writing to accurately reflect God's Word. As David Limbaugh said, in spite of the extreme length of time over which it was written and the large number of diverse authors, the Bible is remarkably thematically integrated.[103]

Christians, and particularly evangelical Christians, believe the Bible is the revealed, accurate, and reliable Word of God. Evangelical Christians believe the Bible is inerrant because it was inspired by God and is objectively true. In the Bible, Christians believe God reveals Himself as a personal God, concerned with each person, and also concerned with His creation corporately. As set out in the Bible, God created man in His own image, meaning that man, while he doesn't look like God since God is non-corporeal, has the same mental makeup as God. Man was given free will by God to make choices and decisions of man's own volition, instead of man simply being an obedient slave. The first man and woman were named Adam and Eve. At the same time (or before) God created angels, or beings designed to serve God. The greatest and most beautiful of the angels was named Lucifer. Lucifer, however, had pride and arrogance and demanded to be coequal with God. War ensued in heaven and Lucifer and one-third of the angels were thrown out, apparently to Earth. Lucifer was then renamed Satan. Satan then tempted Eve and then Adam with the same sin Satan himself was guilty of, hubris, particularly against God. Adam and Eve ate the apple from the tree of the knowledge of good and evil despite an admonition from God not to, and thus committed the original sin. Sin is usually defined as acting outside the will of God. This event is typically referred to as the "fall

---

[103] David Limbaugh, Jesus on Trial, (Washington DC: Regnery Publishing, 2014

of man" since, as the result of Adam and Eve's sin, man, along with the entire creation, fell from fellowship and became separated from God. From the third chapter of Genesis on, the Bible relates God's efforts to redeem His creation from that original sin, finally sending His son, Jesus Christ, to pay the redeeming price on a Roman cross for the sins of all mankind, once for all, and then rise bodily from the dead. Some, if not most, evangelical Christians believe we are currently living in what is called the "Church Age," provided through God's grace, to allow as many people as possible to accept Jesus as their Savior and thus be redeemed to God. At the end of the Church Age, Christ will return to Earth to claim the creation for God once again. Christians believe, as set out in the Bible, in a God of abundant grace, perfect justice, and sure judgment. Christians believe the moral code of the Bible, God's moral code, as set out in the Ten Commandments (Gen. 20:3–17), the teachings of Jesus, such as "Do unto others as you would have them do unto you" (Luke 6:31), "Love your neighbor as yourself" (Mark 12:31), and "Love one another" (John 13:34). Christians believe in not only God, but Satan, whom the Bible describes as the father of all lies and purveyor of all evil. Christians believe in a final judgment, heaven for the saved, and hell for the damned. Humility, repentance, joy, peace, patience, kindness, goodness, faithfulness, gentleness, and self-control (Gal. 5:22) are all considered virtues. God, and Jesus, know no skin color, ethnicity, social status, economic status, power, or position. All are equal in the eyes of God. Finally, at least evangelical Christians believe God is active in the world and is driving history to its conclusion, the details of which are contained in hundreds of prophecies in both the Old and New Testaments and in the Book of Revelation.[104]

The Christian worldview is superior to Humanism and the incorporated philosophies of scientific naturalism and socialism for the following reasons.

Christianity gives meaning, point, and purpose to life. Humanism does not. The theory of cosmic accident dictates that one's life is pointless, no matter how it is lived, and that there is no higher power that cares about the individual. This concept is nihilistic. The Christian God cares deeply about each individual and wants to embrace the last, the least, and the lost. As Dave Ramsey has said, "He's crazy about each one of us." The Scriptures reveal that God wants to bless every one of us with changed and victorious lives. Victory is a much more powerful idea than the Humanist alternative of being happy. Being victorious connotes purpose, success, peace of mind, a race well run, significance, and a meaningful life. Happiness brings up a mental picture of the E-Trade TV commercial, which shows young people partying hard on a huge yacht with the tag line that says "The dumbest kid in your high school class just bought a boat." C. S. Lewis said, "Human history is the long terrible story of man trying to find something other than God which will make him happy."

Christianity offers explanations for the difficult questions and problems in life, and gives life direction to someone seeking a pathway to the future. Few of us have lived very long without encountering ugly and difficult situations, the solutions for which we struggle mightily to find. Jesus, in Scripture, offered the answers and, in the meantime, sent the Holy Spirit as The Comforter. God offers abundant grace to allow us to do what

---

[104] J. Dwight Pentecost. Things to Come, (Grand Rapids: Zondervan, 1958)

we are supposed to. This sounds much more preferable than the Humanist position, which seems to be "work it out for yourself anyway you can. No help is coming."

Christianity is objectively true, very real, and provably so. For people who are dedicated to searching for and finding the objective truth outside of one's own opinion, Christianity reflects reality and absolute truth. The Bible is very real. The people in it really lived and had all the experiences depicted, including the supernatural ones. Christians believe that the Bible is God's Word and contains the absolute truth of the matter. It is the operating manual for people and is full of wisdom and guidance. Humanism, and accompanying philosophies, believe that there is no absolute truth and that what is true depends on how each person views reality and what everyone determines is true for them. In Humanism, the world is ever changing, unstable, and will change. As President George H. W. Bush said, "The truth changed because we have a new reality." The Christian God never changes. He remains the same. His commandments are still the same after 3,500 years. God is consistent throughout the Scripture, which is the complete story of creation from start to finish. The rules don't change in the middle of the game. There might not be anything more stable than Christianity. Which then is the preferable worldview upon which to base one's life? A worldview that is objectively and provably true, stable, and unchanging, or a worldview that is made up by man that is fluid, ever-changing, and unsupported by any objective truth?

A final point revolves around the Humanist idea that humans are basically good and rational beings who, if properly educated, will develop a value system capable of making them productive members of society and help move mankind forward (evolve) toward a peaceful, Utopian society. The Christian viewpoint is just the opposite. Humans are sinful and wicked by nature and cannot earn their way to God. Jesus, God's Son, was a necessary sacrifice and is now a necessary intercessor before God for all sinners who believe in Him. There seems to be a wide disparity between these two belief systems. The Humanist position seems to be eternally optimistic and hopeful, while the Christian position appears quite dark and pessimistic. The objective truth is what the evidence says it is. In this case, history, both what is recorded in the Bible (an accurate history book), and what comes from numerous secular sources, reveals that, with even a cursory glance at the history of Western Civilization, man is anything but the rational, peace loving, and genteel figure that the Humanists like to portray. History is full of war, which is perhaps the ugliest thing we engage in as a civilization. History is replete with astoundingly cruel emperors, egomaniacal kings, murder on a wide, and sometimes officially sanctioned scale, poverty and misery beyond belief, widespread slavery lasting for millennia, purges, pogroms, "the final solution", and just a general total disregard for human life that stains our world with blood and heartbreak. In the twentieth century alone, more lives were lost as the result of war than in all other centuries in recorded history *combined*. The point here is that we are not getting better as the Humanists predict. In fact, we are getting worse, just as the Bible predicts. The simple difference between Humanist relativism and the Christian worldview is that relativists view man as basically good, and Christians view man as basically evil. History supports the Christian view.

In Defense of Christianity

It is difficult to prove a negative. Humanists rely partly on scientific naturalism to create the assumption that there is no God or at least not one worth mentioning. In Humanism, no God is necessary. While Humanists have little proof that there is no God, there is substantial proof that there is a God. There seems to be no other alternatives; either God exists, or He does not. If the universe did not come into being by accident, then it must have been created on purpose by an intelligent designer. There is proof of this. The complexity of the universe, planet Earth, the rest of life, and man himself, lends itself to the idea that the whole of creation has been intentionally designed, rather than simply formed by random chance in the void of space and left to inexorably evolve.[105]

A well-used but good analogy is that of the watchmaker. Suppose a primitive hunter-gatherer walked along one day in his normal environment and found a watch. What might he think? The hunter noticed immediately that the watch was made of shiny, beautiful material, hard and smooth, that he had never seen before anywhere in his environment. He saw that there were hands on the face of the watch that appear to move on their own. After some observation, he noticed that the hands were always in the same position at the same time of the day, which seemingly coordinated with the sun. The hunter can make two choices about the watch. He can conclude that the watch is an accident of nature. He rejects this choice because there is nothing in his environment or experience to even suggest that a moving object made from unknown material that seems to have a purpose could be an accident of nature. The watch shows unmistakably that it was intentionally designed for a purpose. His only possible choice is that there is a watchmaker.[106]

Christians believe they have found and know the watchmaker. God has revealed Himself in Scripture as the Creator

---

[105] Groothuis, Ibid.

[106] Groothuis, Ibid. contingency, complexity, and purpose, 245

of the universe and the active driver of history. Like the watch must have seemed to the hunter-gatherer, from both a macro and micro perspective, our world is so massively complex, so finely tuned, and so thoroughly integrated in its operation that the only logical conclusion that can be reached is the same one the hunter-gatherer reached. There is a watchmaker.

The pivotal event for Christians, and the most pivotal event in history, is the bodily resurrection of Jesus Christ from the dead. Many ideas have been put forth regarding how this event occurred to eliminate the supernatural or miraculous aspects from the equation, and thus prevent God and His Son, Jesus, from being who they really are.[107]

First, a look must be taken at the sources for the information regarding the death and resurrection of Jesus. There is very little dispute as to the fact that Jesus of Nazareth was an actual person who lived in first century Palestine and was executed by the Romans. Historians have a unique opportunity because there are eyewitness accounts of those events and of the resurrected Jesus. It is rare in the history of the Ancient Near East to have credible, verified, eyewitness accounts of anything. Most of our information regarding first century Palestine comes from copies of documents purportedly written contemporaneous with the events. Our extant copies of these documents only exist, sometimes in altered form, hundreds of years later. For example, from the Gospels, we know a great deal more about the life of Jesus than we do about commonly accepted historic figures, such as Alexander the Great or Julius Caesar. The Gospels are a unique collection of first person and near first person accounts

---

[107] Groothuis, Ibid.

of the events of the resurrection.[108] Much has been made by critics concerning the authenticity of those accounts, particularly regarding the eyewitness Apostles, Matthew and John. Criticism centers around the proposition that neither Matthew nor John wrote their accounts and that the Gospels were created later to support the Messiah narrative. The Messiah narrative refers to a theory regarding a long string of conspiratorial activities by many people, including Jesus and the Apostles. It is maintained that first, Jesus, and then the Apostles and others, conspired to falsely present Jesus as the Messiah, as foretold in prophecy, who came to redeem the Jews and all people to God. It is alleged that Jesus simply set Himself up as the Messiah throughout His ministry but made a political miscalculation and got on the wrong side of both the Jewish and Roman powers-that-be and wound up being executed. There is no explanation regarding why Jesus would perpetrate this monstrous fraud. After Jesus' execution, critics maintain that the Apostles and other people engaged in a conspiracy to hide the body, present Jesus as having risen from the dead, and continue the conspiracy far into the future, thus allowing legends, folk tales, and traditions to take over, and then write the Gospels as a reflection of those myths about Jesus. Names of well-known Apostles (i.e. Matthew and John) were added to these stories at a later date to make them seem authentic. There is no rational reason given as to why the early Christians might have done that. [109]

Proof of the authenticity of the Gospels, and therefore the Gospel accounts of the resurrection, comes from both external and internal evidence. The Gospels were widely regarded by the

---

[108] Andreas L. Kostenberger, Scott Kellum, and Charles L. Quarles, The Cradle, The Cross, and The Crown: Second Edition, (Nashville: B&H Academic, 2009, 2016)

[109] Ibid.

first century church as being written by their reputed authors. The authorship of the Gospel of Matthew, by Matthew the tax collector and Apostle, was never seriously questioned until the nineteenth and twentieth centuries. Many accounts by early church fathers attribute the Gospel to Matthew without question. The same is true of the Gospel of John, written when John was likely the only surviving Apostle and was both well-known, likely famous, and much beloved. Mark, as the author of his Gospel, wrote as something of an amanuensis for the Apostle Peter. This also has never really been in question. And Luke, a credible historian, said outright in the first verses of his Gospel, who he wrote for, how he did it, and why. So, the Gospels became what they are partly because the early church recognized them as accurate and authentic and partly because they had Apostolic authority behind them i.e., they were eyewitness accounts by Apostles or near-Apostles.[110] Although much criticism has been written about the consistency between the Gospels, the Gospels themselves are actually consistent between accounts. Criticism has been leveled from two different directions, those being that the Gospels are too much alike to be independent accounts by the named authors (specifically the synoptics, Matthew, Mark, and Luke), and that the Gospels are not enough alike to be accurate accounts. This is, of course, a glaring contradiction. They can't be both.

The claim that the Gospels are contradictory can be explained by simply looking at the reality of the situation. When Jesus was arrested and executed, the Apostles basically ran and hid. Peter denied knowing Christ three times. They were afraid they would be taken to join Jesus on a cross. They

---

[110] Thomas D. Lea and David Alan Black, The New Testament: Its Background and Message, Second Edition, (Nashville: B&H Publishing Group, 2003)

had no idea what happened or what was going to happen. Various people were at the actual crucifixion, but apparently in an on-and-off fashion. The seven words Jesus spoke on the cross are spread out over four Gospels, with one in Luke, one in John, and the other five in all four accounts. Likewise, accounts of resurrection morning are spread out, with the account of Jesus' first appearance to Mary Magdalene found only in Mark and Luke. Then Peter and John finding the empty tomb appears only in Luke and John. If these accounts were identical, questions would be raised alleging collusion or conspiracy. Exact accounts would, in fact, be evidence that there actually was a plot to fabricate the story. The variance in the accounts can be explained by the fact that the Gospels are either first-hand accounts of what each Apostle saw on that day, where they saw it and at what time, or, in the case of Luke, taken from interviews of many people, including the women, who were eyewitnesses of the events. The point is that it should be remembered that the writers of these first-hand accounts need to be located in time and space to understand what they saw, when, and from what perspective. When viewed in that light, there is no real contradiction in the resurrection accounts. Additional credibility lies in the Gospel of Luke, who apparently interviewed everyone who was there that morning who was still living, again with no real contradiction. Finally, all the synoptic accounts are both alike enough and different enough in time and space perspective to demonstrate credibility.

The best evidence for the truth of the resurrection is not, however, what the Apostles said, but what they did. These were not the acts of rational men engaged in a bold-faced conspiracy or fraud. First, for the forty days between Jesus' resurrection and His ascension, it appears that the Gospel writers hid out. Then, as set out in Acts chapter two, in one day the Apostles began to loudly preach the resurrected Lord in public to large crowds. What odd behavior that was for men whom the powerful of society wanted to kill. Further, they dedicated every minute of the rest of their lives to taking the good news of the Gospel everywhere and to anyone who would listen. James, the brother of John, was killed by authorities. Peter was imprisoned at least once and finally likely executed. Paul, with a thirty-year career in the mission field, suffered hardship, beatings, a stoning, and finally was arrested and taken to Rome. Both Peter and Paul were, anecdotally, executed by the Romans. None of these men, or Mark and Luke, had anything to gain. In fact, they lost everything they had, including their lives, to preach the news of the resurrected Christ. This does not sound like any sort of fraudulent scheme or conspiracy. The only rational conclusion that can be made is that the Gospel writers told the truth—Christ rose from the dead.

A few more observations might be helpful. First, many people saw the resurrected Christ. If this were not true, someone would have cried foul on the story. Second, both the Roman and the Jewish authorities took pains to make sure Jesus' body didn't disappear, but it did anyway. The authorities were doubtless desperate to find it. Had Jesus' body simply been stolen, the Romans and the Jews both had ample resources to uncover the plot and find the body. Third, Jesus was dead. There doesn't appear to be a legitimate, reliable medical authority who would say that any man could survive the events of that day, much less fully recover three days later. Finally, C. S. Lewis put it about as succinctly as anyone in *Mere Christianity*, when he said "Either this man was, and is, the Son of God, or else a madman or worse. You can shut him up for a fool, you can spit at him and kill him as a demon, or you can fall at his feet and call him Lord and God, but let us not come with any patronizing nonsense about his being a great human teacher. He has not left that open to us. He did not intend to."

CONCLUSION

Secular Humanism, as a worldview, squarely stands on the shoulders of the dual belief systems of Darwinian evolution as the god of science and the belief in the innate goodness of all mankind. However, evolution fails to hold up to legitimate scientific examination, and the belief in the goodness of man does not square with either history or real-world experience. Further, Humanism is built on other false assumptions as well, those being that there is no Creator, that a utopian society is possible, that there have never been any supernatural occurrences, and that, without any objective moral standards, man can govern himself. All these false assumptions and positions have been addressed.

In contrast Christianity, a two-thousand-year-old worldview, still remains strong, but now on a worldwide basis. The proof for God and creation, the resurrection of Jesus, the existence of evil in the form of Satan, and the timeless truth of Scriptural values have become stronger over the years, partly from necessity as the result of repeated attacks from secular forces. The attacks will continue and, therefore, Christians must stay in the fight and become even stronger. If Christians haven't reached a crossroads between Bible-believing Christianity and the various secular belief systems yet, it is soon coming. About 2,600 years ago, Jeremiah said, "Stop at the crossroads and look around. Ask for the old, godly way, and walk in it" (Jer. 6:16, NIV).

Discussion Questions

1. Is man basically good or basically evil? What does the Bible have to say about it? What does history have to say about it? How does our socio/cultural environment portray people?
2. Is secular humanism (Marxist socialism, etc.) simply a neutral ground between belief systems or is it an active enemy out to destroy Christianity?
3. Would the watchmaker analogy be effective in witnessing to the lost? Why or why not?
4. Should the Bible be interpreted to fit the socio/cultural climate of the time, as some theologians believe?

Chapter 6:

THEODICY: THE PROBLEM OF EVIL

INTRODUCTION

This chapter will explore the frequently asked, but rarely satisfactorily answered, question "Why does God permit, allow, or cause evil?" As Norman L. Geisler put it, "If God, Why Evil?"[111] Most conventional theodicy, the problem of explaining the existence of evil in a God-created universe, asks this question about God and His nature. I will adopt the position of Warfare Theodicy, which is the idea that God does not, and cannot cause evil. Satan does, and constant warfare has existed between God and Satan since the fall of man. I will attempt to answer the question using the only accurate, reliable, and empirical information we have about God, Satan, and the state of man, which is The Holy Bible.

One of the most challenging and perplexing questions that can be asked of a pastor, or just about any Christian, concerns why God allows or causes bad things to happen to good people. Why does God allow profound evil to exist in the world

---

[111] Norman L. Geisler, *If God, Why Evil?* (Grand Rapids: Baker Publishing Group, 2011)

if, as He says, he loves us? And this probing question is typically asked by someone during emotional or physical suffering, or with, sadly, one of the many great evils of history in mind. Many answers have been attempted. Some answers are relatively theologically based, some philosophical, and a few are just plain secular answers. None seem to be satisfactory. Detailing and rebutting the various answers—philosophical, apologetic, or biblical—that have been offered throughout the history of the church would take up many essays like this one. Therefore, this essay will deal almost exclusively with affirmatively proposing a strictly Bible-based answer to the question rather than attempting to debate previous ideas.

Briefly reviewed, previous ideas include:

1. The soul-making theodicy, which maintains, generally, that monumental evil in the world is somehow offset by an ultimate good intended by God both for the sufferers and others that may derive some unknown good from the suffering.

2. The character-building theory, a corollary to the soul-making theodicy, is the idea that God permits evil, characterized by catastrophe, disaster, tragedy, and death, to challenge us to be better, stronger Christians, and to build character.

3. The utilitarian theory, also a corollary of soul-making, contends that God at least permits evil to occur against some people so He can use it later for greater benefit to more people. (The term "utilitarian" means actions or deeds creating the greatest good for the greatest number of people.)

4. Finally, there is the free will school of thought, championed by Alvin Plantinga, that maintains when man was

created, we were endowed with complete (libertarian) free will, which is the freedom to make any choices we desire. Therefore, evil is nobody's fault but our own.[112]

The controversy still rages, and we have all seen and know people who have suffered heartbreaking tragedy and then entirely abandoned God as a result. It is my opinion that this will only get worse as we move toward the end of the age, thus the need for an answer Christians can give to people who are enduring real pain in a real world. I believe we are compelled to give an answer that will, as best as any answer could, satisfy the test set down by Rabbi Irving Greenberg in reference to the Holocaust. He said, "No statement, theological or otherwise, should be made that would not be credible in the presence of the burning children."[113]

I make several assumptions in this essay. It is assumed that God, as described in the Scriptures, created the universe *ex nihilo* and that His nature, as we can know it, is revealed in the Bible. It is also assumed that the Bible is the accurate and reliable inspired Word of God and is inerrant in the original autographs. Finally, it is assumed that the Scriptures are historically, scientifically, and spiritually true.

ON THE NATURE OF GOD

We can know something of the attributes of God, including His nature and His actions, from the Bible. We can know this because we were originally created "in his own image." This term is used three times in Genesis (Gen. 1:26 and Gen. 1:27),

---

[112] Toby Betenson, "Anti-Theodicy", *Philosophy Compass*, 11, no.1, 24 January 2016

[113] Irving Greenberg, *Cloud of Smoke, Pillar of Fire*, (Minnesota: Paragon House, 1989)

the second mention includes both man and woman, and the third is to Noah and his sons (Gen. 9:6). Since God is pure spirit (Isa. 11:2, Isa. 44:3, and Joel 2:28) and never appears in the Scripture in human form, we can conclude that the Genesis account refers not to our physical makeup, but to our mental and emotional makeup. Often called heart, soul, or spirit in the Bible, our soul is who we really are, not just what we look like. For this reason, we can discern something of the character of God and understand God in human terms.

First, God is the all-powerful force who created and controls the universe. He is omnipotent—all powerful. Genesis provides this in the account of creation. Another powerful account of God's omnipotent power is in Job 40:6 to chapter forty-two. It is God who created, not just the flora and fauna, but the whole ecological system of life and the laws of physics and nature that hold the universe together.

God also provides an example of His omniscience in Job 38 to 40:9. God not only had the power to assemble the universe and make the laws of physics and rules of nature that hold the whole thing together, but we also know "God is not dead" because, if he were, the entire cosmos would collapse into chaos. God knows how it all works because He created the natural laws that make it work. If God is both omnipotent and omniscient, He also knows what is in the hearts of men. He knows what we think and what we are apt to do (1 Sam. 13:14, and 1 Sam. 16:7). Further, He knows, and has likely anticipated, the existence of each one of us before birth (Ps. 139:13, Jer. 1:4–5).

In addition, God is timeless, or better put, outside of time. Time exists as an element of the cosmos, even to the point where Einstein set calculations of time in his laws of physics. Time is a thing. God created time Himself on the fourth day (Gen. 1:14). God stands outside both the cosmos and time. He is eternal. God has always existed and always will (Exod. 3:14). God sees the entire span of history, and God drives history to its outcome (Rev. 4-21).

God is also a God of grace and mercy (Exod. 22:27, Luke 2:40, and John 1:14–16) and desires to redeem His fallen creation to himself, not to do it evil. This is evident by the incarnation and subsequent sacrifice of God's Son, Jesus, to make atonement for man's sin (John 3:16). Likewise, God is a God of justice and, ultimately, judge of Satan, evil, and the wicked (Rev. 20).

Finally, God is immutable. He does not change (Ps. 102:24–27, Isa. 46:9–10, and Mal. 3:6). Therefore, God does not act arbitrarily and capriciously, or in a random fashion. Everything He does is according to plan or to further fulfill that plan. It is a common belief among evangelicals that God places obstacles in our way, causes problems of one sort or another, and even brings tragedy and disaster on us to build character, teach us valuable lessons, or make us stronger Christians. This is sometimes called the character-building theodicy. This describes a God who is arbitrary and capricious, wandering around looking for someone to pick on or make suffer. I do not find this teaching anywhere in the Bible. The God of the Bible is anything but arbitrary and capricious and doesn't randomly inflict evil and suffering on anyone in His creation. This leads us to the next section.

ON SATAN

Philosophers say if there is good, then there must be evil. If there is God, who is good, then there must be someone who is evil. The Bible tells us who that is.

God created angels, principally to serve Him. Three angels, Michael, the Archangel (Jude 1:9), who is a warrior, Gabriel, a messenger (Dan. 8:16–26, Dan. 9:20–27, Luke 1:11–20, and Luke 1:26--8), and Lucifer, "morning star and son of the dawn" (Isa. 14:12) are identified by name in the Bible. We know Lucifer better as Satan.

Lucifer, and the events that caused him to become Satan, are described in Ezekiel 28:11–17. Lucifer was a created angel, who was ordained by God to be the guardian cherub, presumably around the throne of God. Lucifer, the angel of light, is described as "The model of perfection, full of wisdom and perfect in beauty" (Ezek. 28:12). Lucifer was apparently far superior than the other angels God created. All angels apparently have the ability to use free will. Ezekiel said, "You were blameless in your ways from the day you were created till wickedness was found in you. Through your widespread trade you were filled with violence, and you sinned" (Ezek. 28:15–16). This was the original sin, committed not by Adam and Eve, but by Lucifer. Lucifer became the author of sin, the progenitor of all evil, and the father of death. Lucifer's sins were hubris, pride, arrogance, and wanting to be God. This is well-recorded in Isaiah 14:13–14, which states, "I will make myself like the Most High." Both Isaiah and Ezekiel document Lucifer, now Satan, as being cast out of heaven (Isa. 14:12, Ezek. 28:16) using some spectacular language, including, "So I drove you in disgrace from the mount of God and expelled you, O guardian Cherub" (Ezek. 28:16), and "How you have fallen from heaven, O morning star, son of dawn!" (Isa. 14:12). And, when Satan was cast out, according to Revelation 12:3–4, he took about one-third of the angels with him. They are typically referred to as demons.

Some interesting terms are used in the passage from Ezekiel 28:16, which gives us a little insight into Satan's character and attributes. The term "trade," according to Charles H. Dyer,[114] connotes "To go around from one to another."[115] The implication here is that Satan was going around to other angels, plotting a rebellion against God, and gaining loyalty with the promise of big rewards. According to James Strong's Concordance,[116] the term "violence" denotes "cruelty, falsehood, and malicious disruption of the Divinely established order of things."[117] In short, Satan was plotting a revolt against God.

These events likely occurred before the creation of Adam and Eve, because Satan appeared in the form of a serpent, which is a beautiful creature in its un-cursed state,[118] and one that could talk, showed up in the garden of Eden and immediately displayed who he really was by convincing Adam and Eve to disobey God and allow sin and evil to enter creation (Gen. 3:1–7). The cause and originator of sin and evil on Earth is Satan.

Satan has other abilities as well. He still has access to the throne of God and can still speak directly to God (Job 1:6–7). We also know that Earth is Satan's domain, according to Job 1:7b, which states, "From roaming through the earth and going back and forth in it." In Matthew 4:1–11, Christ Himself is tempted by Satan. 1 Peter 5:8 also states, "Your enemy the devil prowls around like a roaring lion looking for someone to devour." Satan hasn't given up and hasn't gone away.

---

[114] Charles H. Dyer, *The Bible Knowledge Commentary, Old Testament,* John F. Walvoord and Roy B. Zuck, Editors (Colorado Springs: David C. Cook, 1985) 1284

[115] Ibid.

[116] James Strong, *The New Strong's Expanded Exhaustive Concordance of the Bible* (Nashville: Thomas Nelson, 2010) 99

[117] Ibid.

[118] Charles Caldwell Ryrie, The Ryrie Study Bible, Expanded Edition, NIV (Chicago: Moody Press, 1994) 8

There have been various theological attempts to explain the nature and whereabouts of the Kingdom of God or the Kingdom of Jesus Christ. Some denominations believe that the Kingdom of God exists on Earth since, variously, the Resurrection, the Ascension, or the Day of Pentecost. Without engaging in a large theological debate, Jesus himself said several times that Satan is the "Prince of this world" (John 12:31, John 14:30, and John 16:11). Jesus also said in those passages that Satan is judged and stands condemned. That judgment and condemnation won't take place, however, until the fourth chapter of Revelation, which is when the risen Christ takes the scroll (the title deed to Earth) and prepares to return to claim His kingdom. So, while Christ holds the authority to the kingdom, he has not yet claimed that authority. The Earth is still under the fist of Satan.

Finally, we should look at Satan's weapons in his war against God. We already know, from Ezekiel and the Genesis accounts, that Satan is full of hubris, arrogance, and exceeding pride. He is the ultimate liar, and he's very good at it. He sold apples to Adam and Eve with a big lie. Also, in Satan's tool bag are the necessary implements to produce evil on a monumental scale. In the Matthew account of Christ's temptation, Satan tempted Jesus with complete power and control of the Earth (Mt. 4:8–9). Satan tempts man with greed and power, which is perhaps the same motivations Satan tempted Adolf Hitler with, for example. Satan also uses pride, envy, and wrath. In fact, the traditional list of the Catholic Church's seven deadly sins, taken directly from the Bible, just about takes in all of Satan's weapons used to tempt man in this war. Those seven deadly sins include:

1. Lust: Intense desire for something over and above need (Mt. 5:28, 2Tim 2:22)

2. Gluttony: Overindulgence in something to the point of extravagance and waste (Prov. 23:21).
3. Greed: Rapacious desire (Eph. 4:19, Heb. 13:5, and Mt. 6:19).
4. Sloth: Irresponsibility (Prov. 15:19).
5. Wrath: Self-destructive hatred and anger (Prov. 15:1, Rom. 12:19).
6. Envy: Covetousness (1 Peter 2:1–2, Prov. 14:30).
7. Pride: Hubris (Prov. 16:18)

All seven are powerful tools that Satan uses to produce both sin and evil. All are sins, and it might be noted that all are *attitudes,* not the sinful acts themselves. This suggests to us that Satan is subtle, and works by corrupting people's minds with self-absorption, evil, and self-destructive thoughts, so that we make ourselves walk in the way of sin rather than in the way of God.

ON FREE WILL AND SIN

The concepts of free will and sin are inextricably linked in any discussion of theodicy because one necessarily follows the other and both combine to produce evil. The idea of libertarian free will seems self-evident and empirically demonstrable. Man was created, not as an automaton, but with the ability to choose actions and deeds and be free of compulsion and using his own unfettered volition. There are various gradients of the free-will concept, mostly originating from Calvinism, that would restrict libertarian free-will in one fashion or another. But empirically it is very clear that no restrictions apply to man's choices and decisions since profound evil results from many of those choices, and God could not possibly direct such evil. Therefore, man is completely free to make choices outside the will of God, which is the basic definition of sin. In a good analogy, the Old Testament repeatedly refers to sin as stumbling from the path of righteousness (Isa. 26:7), the straight path (Ps. 27:11), the path of God's commands (Ps. 119:32), the path of life (Proverbs 15:24), and the path of the upright (Proverbs 15:19). In short, sin is acting outside the will of God for our lives. All men sin because all men have the free will to sin. We typically call it human nature or sin nature. God cannot tolerate sin, thus the necessity of Jesus.

Evil itself is frequently divided into two or more types, including man-caused evil and natural evil. We know that man-caused evil is provoked by Satan and caused by sinful men. Natural evil, for most theologians, requires a different explanation, although the explanation seems to be in the Bible. Kent Dunnington[119] stated that the difficulty with warfare theodicy lies in attempting to explain natural evil (hurricanes, tsunamis, volcanoes, etc.). Gregory Boyd[120] counters that argument by stating that while there is a distinction between man-caused and natural evil, this is a distinction without a difference. Boyd states, "Why then should Christians object to blaming the devil for cursing us with a certain aspect of nature...even if we cannot offer a detailed account of how the devil accomplished the cursing and even though the cursing can also be explained in terms of natural causes."[121] Regardless of how Satan did it, in Romans 8:18–22, the Apostle Paul made it perfectly clear that at

---

[119] Kent Dunnington, "The Problem with the Satan Hypothesis", *Sophia*, 57, no. 2, June 2018.

[120] Gregory A. Boyd, *Satan and the Problem of Evil* (Madison: InterVarsity Press, 2001)

[121] Ibid., 276

the fall of man the creation itself was separated from God and also bears the burden of the weight of sin ("bondage to decay").

Boyd[122] also contends (and I agree) that God drives history to its conclusion and ordains certain events to take place regardless of individual free will or Satan's power and influence. Some of these include the fulfillment of the Covenants of the Old Testament, the preservation of the Jews corporately as an identifiable nation, the gift to us of an intact, accurate, and reliable Bible, the incarnation, life, death, and resurrection of Jesus, the fulfillment of numerous prophecies, and the events of the Book of Revelation. Spiritual warfare takes place over the souls of men and possession of creation, and these matters are won or lost on the battlefield. History's course is ordained by God to be completed as it is spelled out in the Bible.

ON WARFARE

Any warfare study will first seek to explain who fought, where the war took place, what weapons were used, and what they fought for. This is also true of warfare theodicy. We are at a loss to analyze spiritual warfare because it is partly fought in a spiritual plane of existence that we know little or nothing of and have not seen. It is also being fought by spiritual beings in that plane, none of whom we have seen, and with weapons that are probably beyond our understanding. We do, however, have a report from that war, made by our war reporter, the Apostle Paul in Ephesians 6:11–18.

A word about our war reporter, Paul, is in order. Paul had substantial experience with the spiritual realm and some of its inhabitants. He was converted to Christianity from Pharisaic

---

[122] Ibid.

Judaism on the Damascus Road by the Risen Christ, whom Paul saw and spoke with (Acts 9:3–9, Acts 22:4, and Acts 26:12). Later, Paul was taken up to heaven, heard and saw inexpressible things, and met a messenger of Satan who gave him an "affliction" (2 Cor. 12:2). Paul spoke frequently to the Holy Spirit and Jesus. The most notable example is the Macedonian Call found in Acts 16:7–10, in which the Spirit of Jesus sent Paul to the West rather than the East. So, Paul, as much as any other person in the New Testament (except Jesus), certainly believed that a spiritual realm existed.

Paul reported from the battlefield in Ephesians 6:10–12, which states:

> Finally, be strong in the Lord and in his mighty power. Put on the full armor of God so that you can take your stand against the devil's schemes. For our struggle is not against flesh and blood, but against the rulers, against the authorities, against the powers of this dark world and against the spiritual forces of evil in the heavenly realms.

Regarding the combatants in this war, it is clear that Paul addressed the Ephesians as participants. So, the combatants are people, particularly believers, against the spiritual forces of evil. Since Satan is the father of evil, we can assume that the rulers, authorities, and powers are part of Satan's army of angels who were thrown out of heaven with him. Finally, from the various appearances in the Bible, God's angels likely play some role.

While Paul defines the evil players as "Spiritual forces of evil" (Ephesians 6:12) we cannot explain a spiritual battlefield that we know virtually nothing of. The only mentions of some type of war in heaven are the accounts in Isaiah 14:12–14, Ezekiel

28:12–18, and Revelation 12:7, which states, "And there was war in heaven." We don't know the nature of that war.

What we do know is that the purpose of the war is for the hearts and souls of men. If the redemption of God's creation, particularly the redemption of people, was important enough for God to send His Son (fully man and fully God), to redeem both Jews and Gentiles, then the ongoing fight must be over the salvation of mankind.

One battlefield in this war, by necessity, must be the mind of man. As stated above, good and evil actions come from the heart and mind of man. Satan is a purveyor of sinful attitudes and lies, which cause men to engage in sinful acts. Satan is not charged in the Bible with forcing someone to commit a sinful act, but simply tempting and encouraging people to do them. In Matthew 16:23 Satan is rebuked by Jesus for causing disruption in the minds of the Apostles. The concept that Satan and his fallen angels, from the spirit world, attack people's minds to cause sinful attitudes and actions was first part of an idea known as middle knowledge. First posited by a Jesuit priest, Luis de Molina, in the sixteenth century, the idea was recently modernized by Gregory Boyd.[123] The idea is that, because God gave us libertarian free will, God cannot predestine, and therefore He does not foreknow the choices each of us will make until we make them. Future events, regarding man's choices, are not fixed. Since man is fallen and sinful, and since Satan is hard at work trying to corrupt God's creation, some of the choices people make will be evil as the result of Satan's influence. We know this empirically. What we don't always realize is that God takes those choices and constantly adjusts the situation to complete His will regardless, after the choices are made and the

---

[123] Ibid.

evil done. God looks at the entire range of choices that a person may make and adjusts His plan to fit the choice that actually is made. We can readily see that there is a tremendous amount of warfare going on between God and the "spiritual forces of evil" (Ephesians 6:12).

Four examples will serve to demonstrate the nature of this fight. The first is the temptation of Adam and Eve in Genesis 3. What we notice about Satan and his weapons is that first, Satan is a liar. Satan intentionally tells a big lie that he knows will appeal to Adam and Eve. Second, Satan is a beautiful creature, not the ugly red guy with a tail, pitchfork, and horns. Satan is beautifully deceptive. Next, we have an example in Job 1:5. This tells us that Satan has access to the entire creation and the throne of God. Satan is an accuser. One of the things he likes to do is point out to God the failures of the Saints. Finally, we have the ultimate acts of hubris by Satan in tempting both Jesus and the Apostles. Satan went toe-to-toe with Jesus in Matthew 4 with an offer of power. Later, he tried to influence the disciples to deter Jesus' plan, in Matthew Chapter 16. So, we see that Satan has a large number of powerful weapons in the fight, all directed at the mind and heart of man, and all designed to appeal to fallen man to make the wrong choice, which is a decision that will lead to disaster and perpetuate evil.

Next, we get to the weapons humans have to use in a cosmic battle that we can neither see nor hear. Almost all are defensive, and Paul's repeated instructions to believers are to "stand your ground", not attack (Ephesians 6:13). Those who have rejected or denied the Word of God aren't in the fight; they already belong to Satan. The defensive weapons, compared to a soldier's armor, include truth, righteousness, readiness, salvation, and the shield of faith. There are two offensive weapons mentioned: the sword of the Word of God (the truth of the Bible), and prayer. In a war over the ideas, values, and beliefs of mankind, we are instructed to take the fight to Satan by prayer and the spreading of the truth of the Scriptures.

CONCLUSION

The above theodicy is not embraced by most Christians and, in fact, numerous denominations, including the mainline Protestants and the Catholic Church, don't embrace it at all. They prefer various modified Calvinist or Armenian theological concepts. Dunnington states, "I suspect [the reason for this] is because of the trend toward disenchantment that is characteristic of secularization. We feel it is superstitious or fantastical to imagine a world and ourselves subject to an army of angelic powers."[124] I would add to secularization by including rationalism, materialism, relativism, and post-modernism. I suspect Dunnington is right, although there is no logic behind believing in a supernatural God and not believing in the remainder of the supernatural powers described in the Bible along with Him.

Perhaps the whole idea of an unseen war that is fought by God against Satan is just plain scary, and people don't want to consider it. But Satan, demonstrating his power to destroy even devout Christians, has provoked recent disastrous scandals in both the Catholic Church and the Southern Baptist Church, which involve inappropriate and illegal sexual behavior. Why, then, can't we even properly identify the real enemy, recognize his power on this Earth, and take the steps Paul suggested to fight back? To paraphrase Paul Harvey, "If I were the devil I would want people to blame God when disaster and tragedy strike. I would be delighted to go unrecognized as the author of

---

[124] Dunnington, Ibid., 265-266

sin and evil. And I would be thrilled if people forgot I existed. In other words, I would like what's going on right now."

Discussion Questions

1. Controversy between conservative and liberal scholars surrounds both Ezekiel 28:11–18 and Isaiah 14:12–14. Do you believe those two passages reflect the kings of Tyre and Babylon or are they about Satan? Why or why not?
2. In Luke 10:18, Jesus said, "I saw Satan fall like lightning from heaven." When do you think this happened? Was Jesus' statement allegorical? Was it a prediction?
3. Do you believe there is a spiritual realm? Why or why not?
4. Do you believe there is ongoing spiritual warfare between God and Satan? Why or why not?
5. Do you agree or disagree with philosopher and theologian Alvin Plantinga, who said that "evil is nobody's fault but our own?" Do you think Satan is somehow behind all evil?

Chapter 7:

THE END OF THE AGE

"Prophecy is history written in advance"
Tim LaHaye

INTRODUCTION AND THESIS

B iblical Eschatology is the theological study of the end times (also called the end of the age or just the end of history). The study of Eschatology largely involves the study and interpretation of biblical prophecy, both realized and unrealized. This study includes the Revelation to John the Apostle given to him by the Risen Christ which is mostly unfulfilled prophecy. Over the last one hundred years or so, there has been an extreme divergence of theological opinion regarding the interpretation of much of the Revelation and of the prophecies and covenants of the Old Testament as well.[125] This great gulf between the two main schools of theological thought are the direct result of the adoption of two different systems of theology—dispensational and covenant—and concurrently two different methods of hermeneutical interpretation—the allegorical method of the covenant theologians and the literal method of the dispensationalists. My thesis is that the application of one method, the

---

[125] Paul Enns, *The Moody Handbook of Theology,* (Chicago: Moody Press 1986, 1994)

literal, results in accurate and consistent interpretation of the Scriptures as a complete whole, while the application of the other, the allegorical/figurative method, results in speculation, mostly by the individual interpreter or reader.

HERMENEUTICS

Hermeneutics can be simply defined as the principle that deals with the discipline of biblical interpretation. Both dispensational and covenant theology are systematic theologies, seeking to interpret and understand the Bible as a whole i.e., God's complete plan for His creation from Genesis to Revelation, beginning to end. Both systematic methods, however, have markedly different hermeneutics and methods for understanding all that God's Word is telling us. These different methods are founded on some very different fundamental assumptions.[126]

Covenant theologians use various derivatives of the allegorical/figurative method. This method is almost as old as the church itself. While the early church understood the Scriptures literally, Origen (185–254), a church father in Alexandria and later Caesarea, first developed the allegorical method of interpretation of the Scriptures in his school in Alexandria. Given to the Aristotelian methods of reasoning, the theologians of Alexandria increasingly sought to use the non-literal, philosophic interpretation of Scripture, partly to conform to the needs and demands of the church organization. Augustine of Hippo (354–430) took this method to new levels, insisting that mystical, figurative, and supernatural interpretation of Scripture must be maintained to satisfy church orthodoxy (in

---

[126] Walter C. Kaiser Jr. and Moises Silva, *Biblical Hermeneutics*, (Grand Rapids: Zondervan, 1994, 2007)

what was then becoming the Catholic Church).[127] This continued throughout the dark ages.

In the case of the covenant theologians, generally the assumptions are as follows: The Scriptures are taken as an ancient literary text and interpreted in that fashion, which is much the
same as one might interpret William Faulkner or James Joyce.
In addition, source and form criticism of the Bible has become
the interpretive method of choice for liberal Bible scholars for
about one hundred years. This was made popular by Rudolph
Bultmann (1884–1976).[128] This method is sometimes referred
to as Allegorism. Dwight Pentecost, quoting Bernard Ramm,
states, "Allegorism is the method of interpreting a literary text
that regards the literal sense as a vehicle for a secondary, more
spiritual and more profound sense." Pentecost continues, "In
this method the historical import is either denied or ignored
and the emphasis is placed entirely on a secondary sense so
that the original words of events have little or no significance.
... It would seem that the purpose of the allegorical method is
not to interpret Scripture, but to pervert the true meaning of
Scripture, under the guise of seeking a deeper or more spiritual
meaning."[129] The first assumption of the covenant theologians
then is that the literal, actual text of the Scripture is not the final
Word of God, and that higher academic interpretation needs to
be applied to discover the real meaning.

The second assumption, like the first, challenges the historical reliability and accuracy of the Bible, particularly the New

---

[127] Mark A. Noll, *Turning Points, 3rd Edition,* (Grand Rapids: Baker Academic, 1997,
2000, 2012)

[128] Andreas L. Kostenberger, L. Scott Kellum, and Charles L. Quarles, The Cradle, The
Cross, and The Crown, Second Edition, (Nashville: B&H Academic, 2009, 2016)

[129] Pentecost, 4

Testament and any prophecy. Basically, the Bible is not regarded as a historically accurate book, but more as a collection of philosophy, literature, and moral teaching.[130]

The third assumption of the covenant theologians is that because of their interpretive methods, the covenants of God in the Old Testament are spiritual in nature, the Jews as a nation are no longer the chosen of God, and the Christian Church is already the recipient of the covenant blessings, particularly because Jesus has already come into His kingdom. This is referred to as "replacement theology" or "supersessionism." Virtually all covenant theologians hold to this belief.[131] Additionally, some covenant theologians do not hold the position that the Bible is inspired by the Holy Spirit, is reliable, or that it is a primary source of history for both the Old Testament Nation of Israel and the New Testament first century Palestine. This includes some doubts regarding the life of Jesus Himself. [132]

Perhaps the final criticism of covenant theology is best summed-up by Pentecost; "The basic authority in interpretation ceases to be the Scriptures, but the mind of the interpreter. The interpretation may then be twisted by the interpreter's doctrinal positions, the authority of the church to which the interpreter adheres, his social or educational background, or a host of other factors."[133]

The Catholic Church lost its religious hegemony through the efforts of Martin Luther, around 1515. Luther insisted that the common people be given the Word of God in their

---

[130] Kostenberger et. al.

[131] Thomas D. Lea and David Alan Black, *The New Testament: Its background and Message, Second Edition,* (Nashville: B&H Publishing Group, 2003)

[132] Kostenberger, et. al.

[133] Pentecost, 5

own language and that it be interpreted literally.[134] The Jews, including the Apostles and Jesus Himself, and beginning in the time of Ezra around 450 BC, read the Scriptures literally. Literal interpretation, however, even during the Reformation, became "shackled with dogmatism and creedalism," as Pentecost said.[135] Only with the work of John Darby (1800–1882), an Irish Bible teacher, and his creation of the theories of dispensationalism has the application of literal hermeneutics to eschatology been extensively studied and used.[136]

The dispensational theologians believe Scripture, including prophecy and the admittedly difficult to understand Book of Revelation, should be taken at its primary, ordinary, usual, and literal meaning. The Golden Rule of dispensational interpretation is, "When the plain sense of Scripture makes sense, seek no other sense." Ryrie states, "Dispensationalists claim that their principle of hermeneutics is that of literal interpretation. This means interpretation which gives to every word the same meaning it would have under normal usage, whether employed in writing, speaking or thinking." [137]

The literal method embraced by the dispensational theologians has a general set of standards to be applied, as would be applied in any academic, legal, or scientific discipline. As summarized by Pentecost, those standards are:

1. The literal meaning of sentences is the normal approach in all languages.

---

[134] Noll, 143 et. Seq.

[135] Pentecost, 7 et. Seq.

[136] Enns, 555

[137] Charles Caldwell Ryrie, The Ryrie Study Bible, Expanded Edition, NIV, (Chicago: Moody Press, 1986, 1994)

2. The greater part of the Bible makes adequate sense when interpreted literally.

3. All secondary meanings, parables, types, allegories, and symbols depend completely on the primary literal meaning of the term.

4. If the nature of the sentence demands, the literal method will yield to secondary interpretation.

5. This method is the only sane and safe check on the imagination of man.

Both Pentecost, in his book *Things to Come*, and Kaiser and Silva, in their text *Biblical Hermeneutics*, present the argument that the Word of God was inspired to be understandable to ordinary people, Jew and Gentile alike. What would be the point of having God's Word if common people could not read it and grasp its message? Finally, most if not all dispensationalists hold the Bible to be the inerrant and inspired Word of God, and to be historically accurate and reliable.[138]

RESULTANT THEOLOGICAL DOCTRINE

> "One of the distinctives of biblical Christianity is that God knows and reveals the future. Only God can do that."
>
> Tim LaHaye and Thomas Ice

As applied to Eschatology and the interpretation of prophecy and the Revelation, two starkly different views of the end times appear. One view, embraced by the covenant theologians, is typically referred to as amillennialism. The other view, held by

---

[138] Pentecost, 10

almost all dispensationalists, is called premillennialism. Both are substantially based on the assumptions stated above and the application of scriptural hermeneutics.[139]

It has been opined that the most popular Protestant (and Catholic) view of Eschatology is the amillennial position. These positions vary widely in their details. There are many and varied versions of amillennialism simply because the belief system is so subjective. Some liberal theological positions cannot be said to hold an amillennial position simply because they are not concerned at all with Eschatology. However, there is a consensus among the mainstream Protestant denominations regarding Eschatological events based on an allegorical hermeneutic.[140]

The first and, according to both Paul Enns and Pentecost, the most important position of the amillennialists is that there will be no one-thousand-year reign of Christ on Earth, as predicted in Revelation 20:1–5. Amillennialists believe the one-thousand-year millennium is both symbolic and ongoing since the resurrection. This is based on an interpretation of Scripture which starts Jesus' Kingdom at the point He was resurrected. Therefore, the Kingdom of God currently exists on Earth. All other Eschatological positions of the amillennialists must coincide with the fact that there is no millennium.[141]

Second, the Revelation itself is generally interpreted as containing a multi-part description of concurrent events regarding the church and the world from the time of Christ's birth until the second coming. This includes the persecution of the church, the birth of Christ, opposition by Satan, the church avenged and victorious, God's wrath on the unrepentant, and

---

[139] Enns, 537-570

[140] Ibid.

[141] Pentecost, 100

the final victory of the church over secularism and unbelief. All of this is said to take place simultaneously and is ongoing from Jesus' resurrection.[142]

Third, amillennialists do not believe that the return of Christ is imminent. Many things must take place before Jesus will return. These include that all nations will be evangelized, Israel will be converted (or at least the 144,000), apostasy, the antichrist, and signs and wonders. The key point to these events is that Jesus won't return until the Gospel is taken to the entire world and everyone, or almost everyone, repents (sort of). In that case, there needs be no wrath and no judgment.[143]

There are two other matters of importance in the amillennial position. The first is, to avoid the literal development and events of the tribulation, the amillennials believe that we are currently living in the tribulation period and that the descriptions of the length of that period are symbolic. Finally, the amillennials see no distinction in the New Testament between God's treatment of the Jews corporately, i.e. as a nation, and His treatment of the gentiles. Since Christ's resurrection, both are treated the same. No distinction is made between the Nation of Israel, as God's chosen people, and the Church of Jesus. This doctrine is called replacement theology (or supercessionism) and holds that all believers (i.e., the gentiles) replaced Israel as the beneficiaries of the Old Testament covenants at the resurrection of Christ. The Jews, in this view, are now just another group of people, and apparently Israel is no longer special. This theory negates the

---

[142] Tim LaHaye and Thomas Ice, *Charting The End Times,* (Eugene: Harvest House Publishers, 2001)

[143] Ibid.

Old Testament covenants to Israel and transfers them, after the resurrection, to all believers.[144]

The dispensationalists take a starkly different view of eschatology, based on the literal method of interpreting the Scriptures. Interpreting prophecy literally, in harmony with the rest of prophecy and the scriptures, interpreting prophecy and the rest of the Bible consistently, and observance of time relationships, leads to a systematic theology which regards God's Word as a comprehensive plan to redeem His creation, and tells us the mind of God as much as we can understand it. This is built on the logic that the Scriptures should be interpreted consistently, from the beginning in Genesis to the end in Revelation.[145] To regard The Scriptures as a 3,500-year-long collection of literature and fragmented historic accounts makes no sense at all.

Dispensationalists, therefore, take the eschatological position of premillennialism. This includes the belief that the unconditional covenants of God in the Old Testament have not been revoked, forgotten about, or transferred from the Nation of Israel, but will be completely fulfilled, as set out in Revelation. Dr. Paul Enns sets out the dispensational distinctions as follows:

1. Jesus will appear twice, once at the second coming (Rev. 19:1-21) and once to receive The Bride in the air (1 Thess. 4:16–17), which is the church in the church age, and which includes all of those believers saved during the church age (1 Cor. 15:51). This is a distinct event from the second coming of Christ. Premillennialists and most evangelical Christians refer to it as the Rapture. This marks the end of the church age and

---

[144] Ibid., 128

[145] Pentecost, 45 et. Seq.

the beginning, or near beginning, of the tribulation described in Daniel 9:27, Daniel 12:1, and Zephaniah 1:15–16. Dispensationalists point out that the distinction in scripture lies in the fact that, at the rapture, Christ appears in the air and does not physically come back to Earth. Christ only comes to Earth once, at the second coming.

2. There will be both God's judgment and wrath poured on those remaining after the Rapture (Rev. 3:10, Rev. 6:16–17, and 1 Thess. 1:10).

3. There are very distinct differences between God's plan for His church (see No. 1, above) and the Nation of Israel (Rev. 14:1–5). The unconditional Old Testament covenants will be literally fulfilled.

4. At His second coming Christ begins a literal one-thousand-year reign on Earth, culminating in the White Throne Judgment and a "new heaven and a new earth" (Rev. 21:1).[146]

Certainly, if one holds to the belief that history is flexible and is in "the eye of the beholder," then a reliable interpretation of Scripture, regarding the Bible as accurate history, is likely impossible. It has been said that our view of history determines our view of Eschatology.

ESCHATOLOGICAL EXAMPLES

"Where does the Bible teach amillennialism?"
— Dr. Thomas Ice

---

[146] Enns, 553 et. Seq.

One of the most disputed passages of Scripture among amillennials and dispensationalists, and the passage that replacement theology depends on, is the Davidic Covenant (2 Samuel 7:4–17). This critical passage is a reply to David regarding the building of the Temple. First God tells David that it will be his son, Solomon, who will build the Temple. The passage continues with what we know to be the Davidic Covenant:

> Now I will make your name great, like the names of the greatest men of the Earth. And I will provide a place for my people Israel and will plant them so that they can have a home of their own and no longer be disturbed. Wicked people will not oppress them anymore... Your house and your kingdom will endure forever before me; your throne will be established forever (2 Sam. 7: 9–11, 16)

The amillennialist position on this passage is that the phrase, "my people Israel" should be taken symbolically, to refer to all church age believers. In addition, this covenant really applies, not to an earthly kingdom, but to a heavenly kingdom of all believers. In short, Israel does not mean the corporate Nation of Israel in the material world, nor does it mean the Jews.

Dispensationalists first put this passage in immediate and historical context. To begin with, the text was written around 930 BC, probably by Nathan. The covenant, or promise by God, is unconditional, requiring no action from David or the Jews to claim the promise, and is an extension and amplification of the original covenant, given to Abraham (Gen. 12:1–3, Gen. 15:1–21, and Gen. 17:1–21). This promise by God was made directly with the Jews as a people and corporate nation. The Jews, not the gentiles, are the covenant people of God throughout Scripture.

The question must be asked as to why God would make this statement to a tenth century BC prophet of Israel and its King if it were a metaphysical allegory and didn't mean exactly what it said. The plain meaning of the words "Israel" and "offspring" (or "seed" in the KJV) and "forever" seem to make perfect sense. Historically speaking, this covenant has not been fulfilled. God must and will keep his promises. So, along with other passages and the historical record of the wholly unlikely restoration of the Nation of Israel in 1948, it becomes clear that the Davidic Covenant means exactly what it says, and that Israel's enemies will be defeated, Israel will be redeemed and gain a permanent home in the land, and Israel will be ruled by Jesus himself (the seed of David).

Another passage that is a hinge point for the amillennialists and replacement theologians comes from the letter of Paul to the Romans. In Romans 11:17–36, Paul talks about an olive tree; he states, "If some of the branches have been broken off, and you, though a wild olive shoot, have been grafted in among the others and now share in the nourishing sap from the olive root, do not boast over those branches." And, at Romans 11:19, "Branches were broken off because of unbelief, and you stand by faith."

It is the position of the amillennialists, in support of the replacement theory, that Paul believed that the Nation of Israel had forfeited its position as the covenant people of God and were replaced by believing Christians. This is to say that Israel corporately had been rejected, just as she had rejected the Jewish Messiah, and that Jesus was only Messiah to believers. The operative term in the above passage is "grafted in."

The standards of interpretation applied by dispensationalists include placing scriptural passages in immediate and historic context to gain a common sense idea of what the passage means. This is particularly important when interpreting writers, such as Paul, who tend to make their points in lengthy discourses. Using these standards leads to just the opposite conclusion from the amillennial position.

Placed in context, it seems likely that the church (or churches) in and around Rome consisted of a combination of Gentiles and Jews. When Paul wrote his letters, he typically answered questions or responded to problems. In the Roman church he likely received questions regarding whether Jews and Gentiles shared the same salvation through faith and grace. Paul gave a thorough, well-reasoned response, as only Paul could do. So, at the beginning of this discourse, at Romans 9:24 Paul said, "I have great sorrow and unceasing anguish in my heart. For I could wish that I myself were cursed and cut off from Christ for the sake of my brothers, those of my own race, the people of Israel. Theirs is the adoption as sons, theirs the divine glory, the covenants, the receiving of the law, the temple worship and the promises." From the present tense in that verse, it seems clear that Israel had forfeited nothing, including the covenants. The question being answered in the entire discourse, according to Ryrie, is "How does this new scheme of righteousness apart from the law relate to the privileged position of the Jews? Have the promises contained in their covenants failed?"[147] Reading further, to the conclusion of the discourse, Paul answers both questions. In Romans 11:25–26 Paul states, "Israel has experienced a hardening in part until the full number of the gentiles has come in. And so all Israel will be saved, as it is written: The deliverer will come from Zion; he will turn godlessness away from Jacob. And this is my covenant with them when I take away their sins." (quoting Isaiah). The Eschatological

---

[147] Ryrie, 1742

implications of this passage are clear; that the covenants, both Abrahamic and Davidic, will be fulfilled corporately in the Jewish Remnant, sealed by God at the end of the tribulation, as set out in Revelation 7:1–8. On a common sense level, a graft is an addition to a tree, not a replacement. The tree still lives, and the graft becomes a part of the tree. Paul expressed the theological concept that, as saved people in the church age, we became, not just God's creation, but part of His family, along with the Jews, who remain the chosen of God.

It is stated five times in Revelation 20:1–6 that, upon His return, Christ's kingdom on Earth will last one thousand years. The amillennial position denies the literal one-thousand-year reign of Christ on this Earth. Amillennialists once again spiritualize the number one thousand and form an allegory that says that Christ began His kingdom in heaven upon His ascension. The amillennialists further believe that the world will (somehow) get both better and worse, even though they believe Satan is currently bound, that the church is currently reigning with Christ, and that Jesus will return sooner or later.[148]

Dispensationalists interpret the one thousand years as one thousand years and regard the millennium as fulfillment of the Old Testament prophecies concerning the post tribulation reign of Christ on this Earth. The only reasonable, common sense reading of Revelation 20 must be that one thousand years means one thousand years. Chapter 20 contains five repeated references to the one-thousand-year period, all used to denote a specific time, and none used symbolically.

Finally, a word must be added about the prophecy of Jesus himself. Jesus' long and final Eschatological prophecy is contained in Matthew 24 and 25. Matthew 24:6–8 states, "You will

---

[148] LaHaye and Ice, 129

hear of wars and rumors of wars, but see to it that you are not alarmed. Such things must happen, but the end is still to come. Nation will rise against nation, and kingdom against kingdom. There will be famines and earthquakes in various places. All these are the beginning of birth pains."

In the interpretation of this passage, the amillennialists hold to one of several nonliteral viewpoints, variously referred to as the preterist, historicist, or idealist views. The preterist view is the predominant choice of modern scholars, although there are overlaps in hermeneutical method. The preterist and historicist views hold the end times prophecies, and the Revelation, are largely about the early church's struggle with the Roman government. Some scholars maintain that the book of Matthew was written after 70 AD to negate the prediction of Christ at Matthew 24:2 that the temple would be destroyed. Through the allegorical method, perhaps most scholars hold to an end times allegory which is vague and ill-defined. This is due to the completely subjective nature of the allegorical/figurative method of the covenant theologians. The historicists regard Revelation and the prophecies as reflecting world history up to the present and the idealists simply see this passage as a symbolic depiction of the timeless struggle between good and evil. Many disparate viewpoints of the passage in Matthew exist among covenant theologians.[149]

A literal hermeneutic, placed in context, regarding the Lord's prophecy produces a startling scenario for today. In context, Jesus answered questions from His disciples, who were clearly upset. The disciples asked three questions in Matthew 24:3, which states, "When will this happen, and what will be the sign of your coming and of the end of the age?" In Matthew

---

[149] Lea and Black, 577, et. Seq.

Chapter 24:6–8, Jesus answered the question involving the end of the age. Christ paints a grim picture in these and subsequent passages about a time far worse than any the world has ever known. The phrases "wars and rumors of wars" and "nation will rise up against nation and kingdom against kingdom" should be a wakeup call or an alarm for us to watch and wait, because these events are already happening. History tells us that more lives were lost in war in the twentieth century than in all other centuries combined. It was the bloodiest century in history. In addition, in 1948, Israel, against all odds, and after 1,400 years of diaspora, was reestablished in the land of Israel, as a nation. Several years ago, an earthquake occurred off the coast of Indonesia which killed approximately 250,000 people. No one had ever heard of an earthquake-caused disaster anywhere near that magnitude. Taken literally, these signs of the end of the age should be of paramount importance to all Christians. Apparently, fanciful speculation by covenant theologians is the rule.

We have seen complete speculation posing as interpretation, when Israel doesn't mean Israel, when land doesn't mean land, when offspring doesn't mean offspring, and when forever doesn't mean forever. We have also seen the clear prophecy of our Lord regarding such a momentous event as the end of the age completely disregarded. It has been suggested by some covenant theologians that applying one's own belief system to the interpretation of Scripture will strengthen one's faith. This is simply man forming God in man's own image, and, as this thesis states, engaging in speculation. Conversely, interpreted using the dispensational, hermeneutical method, done consistently, in context, and in faith, the Scriptures reveal to us God's Eschatological plan for the redemption of His creation.

DISCUSSION QUESTIONS

1. Will "applying one's own belief system to the interpretation of Scripture" strengthen one's faith? Why or why not?
2. Do the Abrahamic, Davidic, and New (Jer. 31) covenants apply to gentiles in the Church Age? Why or why not?
3. Discuss the arguments in favor of each side in the debate between covenant theologians and dispensationalists.

Chapter 8:
ON THE RAPTURE

INTRODUCTION

T his chapter will seek to support the occurrence of the rapture of Jesus' Church before the rise of the Antichrist and the beginning of the tribulation, a pretribulation rapture, as being both a biblical and empirical necessity, and an imperative event that triggers the rise of the Antichrist and the beginning of the tribulation period.

The rapture of Jesus' Church, what it is, when it will happen, and even if it will happen, has been the topic of much debate between the covenant theologians and the dispensationalists over, particularly, the last fifty years or so.[150] The debate picked up steam in 1970, becoming not just an academic, divinity school exercise, but taking on substantial popular appeal with the publication of Hal Lindsey's groundbreaking book *The Late, Great Planet Earth*.[151] Since then, dispensationalism has gained a significantly larger public following, particularly in the UK and US, through the influence of Lindsey, who is still active, and the extremely popular *Left Behind* series of books

---

[150] Charles C. Ryrie, *What You Should Know About the Rapture* (Chicago: Moody Press, 1981) 9-15.

[151] Hal Lindsey, *The Late Great Planet Earth* (Grand Rapids: Zondervan, 1978).

and movies created by Tim LaHaye and Jerry B. Jenkins, beginning in 1995.[152]

Basically, the fundamental disagreement involving eschatology in the Bible between the covenant theologians and the dispensationalists revolves around matters of hermeneutics and interpretation, particularly concerning the literal interpretation of the dispensationalists as opposed to the allegorical method favored by the covenant theologians. Covenant theologians generally read Revelation and the prophecies regarding the end of the age throughout both the Old and New Testaments as figurative or allegorical, while the dispensationalists interpret the whole Bible consistently, as literal and contextual, considering what the author intended to say and what his readers understood him to mean.[153]

In addition to that ongoing fundamental doctrinal difference, Christians of one denomination or another who lean toward the dispensational viewpoint hold at least three different opinions regarding the timing of the rapture. Without going into the complexities of the end of the age, the order of events at the end of the age from a dispensational standpoint are, first, the rise of the Antichrist, which brings on the tribulation period of seven years, the seventy weeks of Daniel (Dan. 9:1–27). In the middle of the tribulation, after three and a half years, the Antichrist becomes a totalitarian despot, defiles the Temple of the Jews, and the final judgment of man and evil begins. This culminates in the Second Coming of Jesus, the end of the age,

---

[152] Tim LaHaye and Jerry B. Jenkins, *Left Behind* (Colorado Springs: Tyndale House, 1995).

[153] Paul Enns, *The Moody Handbook of Theology* (Chicago: Moody Publishers, 2014) 387-425.

and the beginning of the millennial kingdom.[154] This chapter concerns, specifically, when the rapture of Jesus' Church will occur, before the rise of the Antichrist (pretribulation), in the middle of the tribulation (mid-tribulation), or at the end of the tribulation, concurrent with the Second Coming (post tribulation). This chapter takes the pretribulation position and will attempt to demonstrate that there is only one point in time when the rapture could possibly occur, both logically and theologically, and that is before the rise of the Antichrist and the beginning of the tribulation.

THE RAPTURE

Perhaps the most significant statement in the Bible specifically referring to the rapture is found in 1 Thessalonians 4:17–18, which states, "After that, we who are still alive and are left will be caught up together with them in the clouds to meet the Lord in the air." James Strong states that the term translated "caught up" is *harpazo* in Greek (and *rapturo* in Latin) and means to be snatched away quickly. From the connotation of the term, the idea of disappearing instantaneously can be understood.[155] The full statement of Paul describes the entire event, "For the Lord himself will come down from heaven, with a loud command, with the voice of an archangel and with the trumpet call of God, and the dead in Christ will rise first. After that, we who are still alive and are left will be caught up together with them in the clouds to meet the Lord in the air" (1 Thess. 4:16–18).

---

[154] John F. Walvoord, *Revelation* (Chicago: Moody Publishers, 2011).

[155] James Strong, *The Strong's New Expanded Exhaustive Concordance of the Bible* (Nashville: Thomas Nelson, 2010) Greek, 726.

The event of the rapture is described by Paul one more time, in 1 Corinthians 15:51-54, which states, "Listen, I tell you a mystery: We will not all sleep, but we will all be changed –in a flash, in the twinkling of an eye, at the last trumpet. For the trumpet will sound, the dead will be raised imperishable, and we will be changed." We see that the rapture, then, consists of the Risen Christ calling His Church home to be with him in the air, and not setting foot on the ground –this is not the Second Coming of Revelation. This will occur suddenly and include all believers, alive and dead, from the Church Age, which is that period from the Day of Pentecost of Acts 2 to when the time comes for Jesus to remove His Church.

In that regard, the rapture is "imminent." This means that nothing at all must happen. No pre-rapture events have to occur at this time before the rapture can happen. Additionally, the rapture is an event ordained by God. It will happen regardless of any circumstances on Earth. The rapture is inevitable. But imminent does not mean immediate or soon. The first church believed, as apparently Paul did, that Christ's return was both imminent and was going to occur soon. This turned out not to be the case. In fact, the lengthy intervening period of time between the Day of Pentecost and today, called the Church Age (or the Age of Grace) by dispensationalists, is nowhere contemplated in either the Old Testament or the New Testament.[156] But, as will be discussed, we now know, some two thousand years after the New Testament was written, that the events depicted in Revelation involving the rise of the Antichrist and the tribulation can well take place in the twenty-first century, when it would have been both unimaginable and impossible for them

---

[156] John Walvoord, *The Rapture Question* (Grand Rapids: Zondervan, 2011) 11.

to have taken place in the first century, or even in the first half of the twentieth century.

Finally, in Matthew 24, Jesus delivered a long prophecy, complete with parables, regarding the signs of the end of the age. As part of that discourse, Jesus states, "Therefore keep watch, because you do not know on what day your Lord will come. ...So you also must be ready, because the Son of Man will come at an hour when you do not expect him" (Matt. 24:42a and 44). Jesus repeated this once more in Matthew 25:13.

These statements by Jesus, and a few from Paul, give rise to the question of the partial rapture.[157] Popular during most of the twentieth century, the idea of the partial rapture of the church is that only those who, by their persistent watching and waiting, will be taken up in the pretribulational rapture. The rest, apparent backsliders or comfortable Christians, will be left behind. Dwight Pentecost speaks at length about the partial rapture theory,[158] first characterizing it as being one that requires works in addition to faith. Pentecost also criticizes the partial rapture theory as flying in the face of the completed work of Christ, which "is a perfect salvation, by which the sinner is justified, made acceptable to God, placed in Christ positionally, to be received by God as though he were the Son himself."[159] Finally, Pentecost, in his harshest and most telling criticism, points out that the partial rapture theory requires God to judge Jesus' Church, and place part of it in the tribulation period. As will be discussed later, neither this writer nor Pentecost believes Jesus' Church is called to judgment. This supports the position

---

[157] J. Dwight Pentecost, *Things to Come* (Grand Rapids: Zondervan, 1958) 156 et seq.

[158] Ibid., 156-163.

[159] Ibid., 160.

that the entire church will be removed before the judgment of the tribulation occurs (1 Thess. 4:13–18 and 1 Cor. 15:51–54).

The Church

At this point, a brief explanation of what the Church of Jesus Christ consists of and how that church is regarded by God is in order. R. G. Clouse offers a beautiful definition of the church as it exists in the church age. He said, "Thus the church is the spiritual family of God, the Christian fellowship created by the Holy Spirit through the testimony to the mighty acts of God in Christ Jesus. ...Wherever the Holy Spirit unites worshiping souls to Christ and to each other there is the ... church."[160] Included in the body of the church, then, are all true believers in Jesus as Messiah.

There are some important attributes to note regarding Jesus' Church. The Church, consisting of all believers beginning at least from the Day of Pentecost, is Christ's most prized possession. Jesus loves His Church (Matt. 16:18, Acts 20:28, Eph. 5:23, Col. 1:18–20, and Col. 1:24). The Church, particularly in Revelation, is referred to as "The Bride" (Rev. 19:6–8 and Rev. 22:17). Jesus made the ultimate sacrifice specifically for all who would believe, i.e. The Church (Rev. 1:5–6). And the whole point of the church age may be to allow time for all who would to believe and become part of Jesus' Church and further the work toward redeeming God's creation. Finally, Jesus sent the third part of the triune God, the Holy Spirit, on the Day of the Pentecost, with specific work to do, including to reside with each believer and to act as counselor and the Spirit of Truth who

---

[160] R. G. Clouse, *Evangelical Dictionary of Theology*, Walter A. Elwell, Editor (Grand Rapids: Baker Academic, 2001) 246.

will "teach you all things and remind you of everything I have said to you" (John 14:15–26). Ryrie summarizes the various aspects of the Holy Spirit, taken from the Book of John, stating that the Spirit will convince the world of sin, righteousness, and judgment, and teach the believers the truth.[161] Paul added that the results of the Spirit in believing Christians would be "Love, joy, peace, patience, kindness, goodness, faithfulness, gentleness, and self-control" (Gal. 5:19–22). These are virtues that we all desperately need, and Christ is more than willing to grace His sinful but believing Church with those virtues. Finally, as stated emphatically by Paul in 1 Thessalonians 4:13–18 and 1 Corinthians 15:51–54, Jesus will call his Church home before the tribulation.

THE RAPTURE AS IMPERATIVE

The Scriptures

This chapter contends that the rapture of the Church of Jesus before the tribulation period is both necessary and imperative. Along with empirical and common-sense reasons for this, there is substantial biblical support for this proposition.

First, in 1 Thessalonians 4:15–18, quoted above, Paul speaks of the Lord coming in the air to call His Church home and meet it in the air. In the extended version of this passage, 1 Thessalonians 5:1–4, Paul points out that this event, the rapture, will be sudden, without warning, "Like a thief in the night." But Jesus, in Matthew 24:4–31, offers detailed warnings and signs of His coming when He says, "For as lightning that comes from the east is visible even in the west, so will be the coming of the Son

---

[161] Charles Caldwell Ryrie, *Ryrie Study Bible, Expanded Edition* (Chicago: Moody Press, 1994) 1648.

of Man....and all the nations of the earth will mourn...." (vss. 27 and 30). This event, described by Christ, cannot be the sudden rapture of the Church but the Second Coming of Revelation in chapter 19. Paul reaffirms the suddenness of the rapture in 1 Corinthians 15:51–52, which reads in part, "In a moment, in the twinkling of an eye." The two events described are much different in character and point to a rapture of the church prior to the events of Revelation, when Jesus will actually touch down and bring His presence and His kingdom to Earth.

Next, it must be pointed out that the Church nowhere appears as being on Earth during the events of the tribulation, from Revelation 4 to 20. Critics say that this is an argument from silence and is therefore not particularly convincing. The argument from silence becomes much more convincing because the Church is the main focus of attention in the first three chapters of Revelation, and then simply disappears from the narrative as soon as the scene shifts to heaven, the scroll is opened by the Lamb, and judgment on the Earth begins. Logically, it appears that the Church has been removed from this judgment. This argument is bolstered somewhat by Revelation 3:10 in the view of some scholars in that Christ says to the church at Philadelphia, "Since you have kept my command to endure patiently, I will also keep you from the hour of the trial that is going to come upon the whole world to test those who live on the earth." This verse can be thought of not only as a literal message to the church at Philadelphia but an indication and a prophecy that Christ will remove the faithful from the judgment of the tribulation.

Finally, two passages in Revelation, both hotly disputed, may reveal the Church is already in heaven during the tribulation. The first passage is Revelation 5:8–10, which depicts twenty-four elders in heaven, falling before the Lamb. These elders are thought by some to represent the Church already in heaven at the beginning of the tribulation. This thought is partly supported by the fact that no other likely identification of the twenty-four elders makes much sense. The twenty-four elders appear again in Revelation 11:16 and Revelation 19:4. The second passage is Revelation 4:9–10, depicting the "souls of those who had been slain because of the word of God and the testimony they had maintained." Some dispensationalists believe these souls to be people who were evangelized and then killed early in the tribulation while others believe these are all the church age martyrs caught up in the pretribulation rapture.

Walvoord[162] talks about the church age and the rapture depicted in the parables of Jesus in Matthew 13. The parables generally relate to the kingdom in the church age, and to the judgment to come at the end of that age. What is important to note about these parables, particularly *The Wheat and the Weeds* in Matthew 13:24–30, and *The Net* in Matthew 13:47–50, is that they depict a separating by Jesus' angels of the righteous from the wicked (the good fish from the bad and the wheat from the tares) but report only judgment for the wicked, suggesting the Church will not go through the tribulation. Finally, Walvoord mentions the well-known passage in John 14:1–3, which states, "Do not let your hearts be troubled. Trust in God; trust also in me. In my Father's house are many rooms; if it were not so, I would have told you. I am going there to prepare a place for you. And if I go and prepare a place for you, I will come back and take you to be with me that you also may be where I am." Two things point to a pretribulation rapture in this passage. The first is that Jesus begins the passage with a very comforting thought, suggesting that there will be no tribulation for the Saints. The

---

[162] Walvoord, *The Rapture Question*, Ibid., 182-195

second is that Jesus describes coming for His Saints but does not put this coming in anywhere near the dramatic context he does in Matthew 24. Jesus, in a very gentle fashion, is simply coming to take His Saints home.

EMPIRICAL AND COMMON SENSE MATTERS

The State of the Planet

The Apostle Paul spoke a great deal about the idea of a revealed mystery. In fact, the term "mystery" appears twenty-one times in Paul's letters alone, and there are twenty-eight total uses in the New Testament.[163] The well-known passage in 1 Corinthians 15:51 is just one example of Paul revealing to the Church a previously hidden, or unknown truth. S. Motyer states that a mystery, as the term is used in Scripture by Paul, indicates something that God has revealed to us that was previously unknown and unknowable.[164] This is certainly true of the rapture passages in Corinthians and Thessalonians. It may also be true of the contents of the Book of Revelation. The church of the first century held to the simple idea that Jesus was coming back soon. As Revelation was written late in the 1st century, around 90 AD, they most likely had not read it. Even if they did, they still apparently held a rather unsophisticated view of the complicated goings on in the book and its relation to the Old Testament and New Testament prophecies. Later, an allegorical interpretation of Revelation and most of the rest of the Bible was adopted by the church, beginning with Origen and Augustine. Only in the nineteenth century, originally through the work of John Darby (1800–1882), did the systematic theories of dispensationalism

---

[163] S. Motyer, Evangelical Dictionary of Theology, Ibid., 803.

[164] Ibid.

begin to come back into prominence, including the various theories of the rapture. The conservative element of classical dispensationalism has been well supported in the twentieth century and into the twenty-first century by the scholarship of Lewis Sperry Chafer, John Walvoord, D. I. Schofield, Charles Caldwell Ryrie, Dwight Pentecost, Thomas Ice, and others, while the popular version, notably by Hal Lindsey and LaHaye/Jenkins, has exposed many, many people to the same beliefs. The point is that only recently have we been able or even capable of gaining a much fuller, systematic understanding of the mysteries of the prophecies, the rapture, and the end times. This probably is as it should be, because only now, in about the last twenty-five years, can we fully understand that the fantastical and frighteningly violent events depicted in the tribulation could take place for real. The rise of the Antichrist and the events of the tribulation are now a real possibility, not just something that could happen in the far distant future. The technology is all there for the entire world to view in real time the two witnesses preaching, dying, and being taken to heaven by God (Rev. 11:1–14). Everything necessary is in place to compel the entire world to take the mark of the beast (Rev. 13:16–18) and be unable to conduct commercial transactions without that mark (Rev. 13:17b). Everything is in place, all the organizations, communications, funding, and political consortiums for the Antichrist to take control by diplomacy of the entire government, particularly of the Western World (Rev. 6:1–2). All the necessary, highly destructive military power is now at our disposal for the Antichrist to force his rule on the nations and wage effective warfare on a global scale against all who oppose him (Rev. 6:3--). And all is in place for a global communications network for propaganda and population control (Rev. 13:7–8). Everything that is needed, including the necessary technology and a global financial market, has been done to provide the opportunity for global control of the world's capital and economy (Rev. 18:1–24). And great strides have been taken to create the one world church for the worship of the false messiah, the Antichrist (Rev. 17:1–18). So, Jesus' return is truly both imminent and probably soon, because literally nothing has to happen for the events of the tribulation to unfold except one thing—the rapture of the Church.

THE NECESSITY OF THE PRETRIBULATION RAPTURE

This paper maintains that, for all the above events to occur, the pretribulation rapture is both imperative and necessary. There are three important reasons for this—two Scriptural and the other empirical—based on observation and practical experience. They are:

1. The tribulation is about judgment. God, through the Risen Christ, will pour out His wrath on the wicked Earth and the impostor Antichrist, will defeat sin and evil, and restore the Kingdom on Earth. Beginning in Revelation 4, when Christ, the Lamb that was slain, opens the scroll, the apocalypse and judgment begins. As we have seen, the Church, all believers of the church age, are more precious to Jesus than anything and Jesus loves His Church. In addition to that, the Scriptures tell us that Jesus has already atoned for our sins, that they are paid for in full, and that, when God looks at us, He sees only His perfect Son who paid that price and who is spotless before God. God does not see our personal sins. There is nothing to judge. R. Youngblood, referring to judgment in the common sense as condemnation,[165] put it succinctly when he said, "Because

---

[165] R. Youngblood, *The Evangelical Dictionary of Theology*, Ibid., 639.

we are born in sin and cannot live up to God's righteous standards, condemnation...hangs over our heads (Rom. 1:18, Eph. 5:5–6, Col. 3:5–6, and Peter 2:3). God himself is the one who condemns. His condemnation is based on his justice, and such condemnation is deserved (1 Kings 8:32 and Romans 3:8). Condemnation comes to the wicked and unrepentant (Matt. 12:41–42, Luke 11:31–32, and John 5:29) and results in eternal punishment, but no New Testament believer who trusts in Christ will be condemned. Jesus came to save rather than to condemn (John 3:16–17) and he frees us from final condemnation (Rom. 8:1–2)." Judgment connotes a finding of liability, guilt, or sentencing for a crime—all negative. At the rapture, there is no guilt to be found in Jesus' Church. The Church cor porately and individually is the Bride of Christ and is perfect in every way. There does not appear to be any hint of a judgment here. Further, why did Christ die on the cross if the Church will be judged for their sins anyway?

Paul states, "For we must appear before the judgment seat of Christ (the *Bema*), that each one may receive what is due him for the things done while in the body, whether good or bad" (2 Cor. 5:10). This concept, the idea of the *Bema*, is repeated several times in Paul's letters. This writer believes the idea of a judgment of some sort is a misunderstanding of what Paul described. In Romans 8:1, Paul states, "Therefore, there is now no condemnation for those who are in Christ Jesus." This affirms Youngblood's discourse on judgment and condemnation. If there is no possibility of condemnation, then there is no judgment at all. This is not a judgment the way the White Throne judgment is portrayed, for example, in Revelation 20:11–15. The White Throne judgment is portrayed as a finding of eternal guilt or innocence. What Paul is trying to portray is an *awards ceremony*, not a judgment. The *Bema* event shares with Christ the joys of heaven given to us for being part of God's family. This is better portrayed in Romans 8:17, which states, "Now if we are children, then we are heirs –heirs of God and coheirs with Christ, if indeed we share in his sufferings in order that we may also share in his glory." Galatians 4:7 states, "So you are no longer a slave, but a son; and since you are a son, God has made you also an heir." Also, Jesus, in Revelation 2:10, promises the "crown of life" to those who will suffer persecution. Again, this is an awards ceremony for God's family, not at all the kind of judgment that is poured down on the Earth throughout the period of tribulation. Finally, Paul (in Romans) spends a great deal of time and writes a very sophisticated discourse proving all the things Jesus has done for all believers on the cross. Paul lists those things as redemption, justification, sanctification, propitiation, and substitutionary atonement. Considering this extraordinary analysis by Paul, it would significantly detract from what Jesus actually did on the cross to suggest that there will be some sort of judgment imposed on Jesus' Church. Therefore, it seems imperative that the Church be removed from the world prior to the worldwide judgment and apocalypse of the tribulation.

2. Further, the Church must be out of the way before the Antichrist is able to rise to the level of power he attains. In fact, the Antichrist would probably not be capable of rising to the position of power he will gain if the Church is still in the world. To begin with, two Bible passages support this position. The first is Matthew 5:13–14, which is the Sermon on the Mount, and Jesus states, "You are the salt of the earth." (13a) and "You are the light of the world." (14a), and 2 Thessalonians 2:7 and 9: "For the secret power of lawlessness is already at work; but the one who now holds it back will continue to do so till he is taken out of the way...The coming of the lawless one will be in accordance with the work of Satan displayed in all kinds of counterfeit miracles, signs and wonders."

It is clear here that, at some point during or before the time of the Antichrist, the Holy Spirit himself will be removed, possibly from Earth altogether. And if the Holy Spirit is gone, so is the Church. In combination, the Church and the Holy Spirit are the "light of the world" and "the salt of the earth." So, it is likely, just from these verses that before the Antichrist can take power and exercise all of his seemingly superhuman skills, the Holy Spirit, who is now preventing him from doing so, and therefore the Church along with the Holy Spirit, will be absent.

3. Finally, there is an empirical argument. This argument is based on observation and experience, and supports the idea that the pretribulation rapture is a necessity for the Antichrist to rise to power and is, in fact, the triggering event that allows the Antichrist to do so.

The US is a unique nation, different in all significant respects from any other nation that exists now or has ever existed. To the founders of our Republic, the history of the church and its relationship to the various European governments were current events. They were well aware of the atrocious nature of church involvement in government and sought to create an entirely new form of government, based on Judeo/Christian ideas, values, and beliefs, and the self-evident freedom expressed in the Declaration of Independence. In this regard, and together with the other political documents, our Bill of Rights was enacted, securing, among other things, the six separate rights contained in the first amendment—no state religion, freedom to exercise our religion, freedom of speech, freedom of the press, freedom to assemble, and freedom to petition our government. These rights don't belong to the government and weren't given to us by our government. They are reserved to the people and cannot be taken away. So, without engaging in a lengthy political science discourse, suffice it to say that our nation was founded, and still exists as the only nation that has ever existed, in which the sovereignty of the nation and the rights of the people, including our first amendment rights, rest in the people alone.

Currently, the US is the wealthiest and most powerful of all nations. This has been the case since, arguably, right after the Civil War. We are also the third most populous nation in the world, behind only China and India. Our economy, which embraces capitalism and is protected and bolstered by our military strength, is likely the largest in the world and has a global impact daily. Our socio/cultural influence, particularly in the broad communications media, also has a significant worldwide impact.

All this being the case, our current political climate is much more polarized than this writer has ever seen in his lifetime and as devoid of any hope of compromise as any in our history, except for the ten or so years just before the Civil War. On one political side are the conservative leaning voters, in control of about thirty states in 2016 and just shy of fifty percent of the popular vote in that national election. On the opposite side are the liberal leaning voters, in control of twenty states and with just slightly more than fifty percent of the popular vote in the 2016 election. Included in this are the sharply divided extremes of both factions. On the right are the capitalists and constitutional conservatives and, remarkably, about eighty percent of the evangelical voters. On the left, which now makes up a significant portion of the Democrat party, are the economic and ideological Socialists.

A word about Socialism is in order. From the relatively straightforward economic theories of Karl Marx, modern

Socialism, over the last 150 years, has progressed to a full-blown socio/economic and political ideology, encompassing all facets of life in the US. Socialism is godless, preferring public allegiance to the service of a strong central government, which dictates the morals to which society will adhere. It is overtly hostile to organized religion of any type, particularly the conservative and evangelical types. Socialism, as we are seeing now, chafes under the restrictions imposed on the power structure by the Constitution and especially the Bill of Rights. The idea behind modern Socialism is not to secure the rights and freedoms of its citizens but to obtain complete power to control its subjects to serve the interests of the government. In short, Socialism is the opposite of both Judeo/Christianity and the founding values of our Republic.

Finally, a look at some demographic numbers is important. Several recent studies, taken conservatively, suggest there may be as many as 240 million nominal Christians in a population of about 340 million. Taking a very cautious extrapolation of that number based on the current membership of the Catholic Church, the Southern Baptist Conference, and several additional mainline Protestant denominations, we can make a rough guess that there are currently about one hundred million believing Christians in the US, slightly less than one-third of the total population. This number could be much larger or much smaller. The true taker of this census, God, is the only one really qualified to make that determination.

It is, in this writer's opinion, highly unlikely, despite any short-term political situation, that there could be a complete surrender of the sovereignty of the US by any political leader or leaders or any political party or other faction, nor could there be a complete suspension or abrogation of the US Constitution or any part of the Bill of Rights, allowing the Antichrist to take political control of the US. There are simply too many people diametrically opposed to any such thing. As it stands, the rise of the Antichrist to control a one-world government seems unlikely without the cooperation of the US.

Now picture a US where, suddenly, in the "twinkling of an eye," one hundred million people simply disappear from our nation. And these won't be just any one hundred million people, they will be all of our believing Christians. Then look at who will be left behind. With the pretribulation rapture, the entire economic, social, and political power structure will have been changed in a moment. At that point, the population of the nation will likely be overwhelmingly socialist and, by definition, godless.

Therefore, when the event of the rapture occurs, it is not at all hard to picture a scenario in which the Antichrist will not only be able to assume totalitarian power over the wealthiest, most technologically advanced, and strongest military nation in the world but will, in fact, be welcomed by most of the people left in the US, regardless of where the Antichrist is actually from. The pretribulation rapture acts as the necessary, imperative triggering event that marks the beginning of the end of the age.

CONCLUSION

This chapter has set out the proposition that the pretribulation rapture is necessary, imperative, and causes the rise of the Antichrist for three reasons, which are:

1. There will be no judgment of Jesus' Church, and Revelation is all about God's judgment on the wicked Earth. Therefore, the Church must be removed before God's wrath can be poured out.

2. The Antichrist will rise only when the salt of the Earth, and the Holy Spirit, are removed, clearing away all spiritual opposition to a one world church, one world government, and totalitarianism.

3. Politically, economically, and militarily, the Antichrist will only be able to take control, particularly of the West, when the US suddenly loses about one-third of its population and falls into chaos, becomes socialist, gives up its Constitution, rights and sovereignty, and voluntarily and willingly agrees to such an arrangement.

Regarding matters like these, dealing with the end of the age, the Apostle John stated in his prologue to the Book of Revelation, "Blessed is the one who reads the words of this prophecy, and blessed are those who hear it and take to heart what is written in it, because the time is near" (Rev. 1:3).

Discussion Questions

1. Do you agree that the End of the Age is very near?
2. Do you agree that the US is not mentioned in Revelation and that all Christians must be out of the way before the Antichrist can take power? Is the Rapture a necessity, then, for the Antichrist to come to power?
3. If you don't agree with, or aren't so sure about the pretribulation Rapture, discuss and explain when the Rapture will occur.

Chapter 9:
ON JESUS AND THE CROSS

"Jesus said, 'It is finished.'
With that he bowed his head and gave up his spirit."
John 19: 30b

What did Jesus mean by "It" was finished? What was finished? What mission or purpose did Jesus have that he finished? We typically don't look at this, the most important and significant occurrence in history, as being over until the women discover the empty tomb three days later. To us, the most important event in history, and particularly for Western Civilization, is the empty tomb, not the cross. While this is true, Jesus accomplished his purpose on the cross. The Resurrection was the final proof of the prophecies and proof to all men that Jesus is Messiah, Son of God. The mission was accomplished on the cross. That's where the mission was actually finished. So, what was finished? What did Jesus mean when He said "it..."?

THE LAW

Let's first be clear about our terminology. The Laws of Moses (the Law) and the Ten Commandments are not the same thing. The Laws of Moses, generally found in Exodus, Leviticus, and Deuteronomy, were given to the Jews by Moses, as inspired by

God, to allow the Jews to be "separate people" and to govern both their religious worship and their civic life the way God wanted them to. The Laws were regarded by the Jews as being somewhat flexible, depending on the exigencies and circumstances at the time. In fact, particularly during the second Temple period (450 BC - 70 AD), the Jews added considerably to the Law, making it so complex as to be ridiculous to the extreme, and almost impossible to follow (Matthew chapter 23). The Ten Commandments, however, were passed down directly to the Israelites by God and carved in stone. They were not optional, subject to interpretation, or in any way flexible. They are commandments from God to everyone at all times. Jesus reaffirmed the Commandments several times and they still apply to us today.

First, Jesus completed the Jewish Law. Jesus said, "Do not think I have come to abolish the Law or the Prophets; I have not come to abolish them but to fulfill them" (Matt. 5:17). Embracing Jesus as Messiah meant that Pharisaic obedience to the law was no longer necessary or efficacious to gain salvation. Sacrificial Temple worship was over. This is what Jesus meant by "fulfill." After Jesus died on the cross, obedience to the law was no longer effective. Temple worship, and all forms of legalism, even now, detract from what Jesus did on the cross.

Basically, sacrificial Temple worship was established by God to allow the Jews to accomplish several things. As Paul set out in Romans, the Temple and accompanying religious observances were designed for redemption, salvation, sanctification, propitiation, and atonement. The Jews most important and serious annual observance is the Day of Atonement, which is held in late September or early October. During that ritual, the chief priest takes the blood sacrifice and pours it on a goat. The goat is then led out into the wilderness and released. This is where we get the term "scapegoat." The goat carries away the sins of the entire nation of Israel for the entire past year. In other words, this is the annual act of atonement for sin.

In 70 AD the Roman General, Titus, as the result of a Jewish revolt started in 66 AD, surrounded the Temple and took it over and killed everyone inside. He then burned the Temple and dismantled it, stone by stone, just as Jesus said (Matt. 24:2). Personally, I believe God ordained this event to happen long before it did to demonstrate to the Jews, and everyone else, that sacrificial Temple worship was over. Legalism was over. Ritualism was over. Works-oriented salvation was over. The final sacrifice had already been made on the cross, one time, for everyone who would come to Jesus. There was and is no substitute and no alternative. Jesus atoned for our sins, then, now, and to the end of the age, on the cross. He was the only one who could.

In like fashion, works-oriented salvation, legalism, and any other rules and regulations designed to restrict admission into Jesus' Church, save repentance and belief, were finished on the cross. After Jesus died on the cross, legalism was no longer effective in gaining one's salvation. God's plan is clear. It was impossible for man to reach up to God on his own and achieve his own salvation. The Jews proved this for 1,400 years under the law, failing miserably time after time. The Jews couldn't even keep the First Commandment because they ran after Baal, Asherah, and a host of other pagan gods that looked like they might be a lot more fun. For God to redeem His creation, God had to reach down to man, provide His own sacrifice, Jesus, to atone for man's sin, and secure a way, one time and once and for all, to reconcile man to the Creator.

That is the message here. We cannot work our way up to God. We are all failed sinners. This is clearly the idea from both the Old and New Testaments. No amount of church activity, kindness to the poor, rituals, confessions, and other requirements—most of which result in guilt, shame, and fear—can get us anywhere near God. This doesn't mean that we should not act like Christians and display those virtues that both Jesus and Paul talked about. We certainly should embrace the attitudes and belief system of the Bible. But the legalism, the rules and regulations, the list of expected duties, and mandatory compliance with standards of behavior being imposed in some churches right now, fly directly in the face of what Jesus did on the cross, and drive people away from our churches and from understanding the real message (Matt. 23:13–14).

SATAN AND EVIL WERE FINISHED

We know Satan is still very active and there is great evil in the world (1 Pet. 5:8). In fact, the twentieth century was the bloodiest century in world history. This is truly shocking, but more people were killed in warfare and from related causes in the twentieth century than in any other. We are not getting better, as some philosophers and theologians believe. We are getting worse—a lot worse. While the battle still rages to its climax, the war was won on the cross. The war, the ongoing desperate spiritual warfare for the souls of men, will continue unabated until the Rapture and the End of the Age. Satan is fighting a vicious, last-ditch, all-out war to take as many souls to hell with him as he can and to destroy God's creation. He has already lost. Jesus stated at least three times that Satan stood condemned and would be driven out. (John 12:31, John 14:30, and John 16:11). Satan unsuccessfully tried to tempt both Jesus and his disciples (Matt. 5:8) to keep Christ from carrying out his mission. Satan failed. Finally, there's no doubt that Satan plotted to have Jesus executed, hoping that would put an end to it, and make Satan lord over God's creation. Satan lost at the resurrection.

After the Ascension, the Kingdom of God, something of a controversial topic, resides where Jesus resides, at the right hand of God. Some authorities and denominations hold that the Kingdom came to Earth when Jesus was born, or some variation on that theme, and that God's Kingdom is now with man. This is not what the Bible says, however. The Kingdom is not a geographical location. The Kingdom is where the King is. The King *is* the Kingdom. The Book of Revelation, if taken at its word and read for what it says, demonstrates this abundantly. This begins when Jesus, the Lamb that was slain, takes the scroll, the deed title to Earth, and opens it. Only Jesus, the King, can do this. Judgment begins and Satan is eventually judged and thrown into the lake of fire forever. Not only is Satan vanquished, but Satan is also already vanquished because, while he has not yet taken possession, Jesus owns the Earth and all of God's creation.

MAN'S SIN DEBT WAS FINISHED

This includes mine, yours, and everyone who will come to Jesus. The statement "It is finished," in Greek, is "*Tetelestai.*" *Tetelestai* is actually a commercial term and was used by the Greeks on commercial documents to indicate that the debt owed was paid in full and canceled as if it never existed. This is the meaning of the term "atonement". The debt had to be paid. It was paid by Jesus on the cross for everyone's sins who would believe in Him, then and now. Nothing you or I do can pay that debt. But now, when God looks at us, all sinners, all He sees is His sinless Son. The debt has been canceled as if it never existed because it was finished on the cross.

God's Plan

Finally, God's plan to redeem His creation was finished on the cross. C.S. Lewis said, "Human history is the long and terrible story of man trying to find something other than God which will make him happy." Lewis was right. A thirty-thousand-foot look at the Bible shows that God revealed who He is to His creation and us. The fall of man was the result of the efforts of Satan, and Adam and Eve "trying to make themselves happy". The entire scope of the Bible is one with the overriding purpose of telling the story of God trying to redeem His creation from the separation from Him that sin had caused. He repeatedly showed grace and mercy to the Jews, who failed every time and finally even rejected their own Messiah. Finally, when it was clear that the Jews could not follow the Law of Moses and the Commandments but had perverted the law for their own selfish desires, God sent Jesus, fully God and fully man, in human form to make the necessary sacrifice for man to finally redeem God's creation to Him. Jesus was the only solution to the problem. Nothing else could satisfy and atone for the sin debt and bring man back to the God who created him. Jesus finished that plan on the cross. We now live in what has been called the Church Age or the Age of Grace. Both names are accurate. At some point, perhaps when Jesus began His ministry, more popularly on the Day of Pentecost (Acts 2), a time began on God's calendar, allowing as many people as possible to repent and believe Jesus is Messiah. Jesus has built His church in what is now about a two-thousand-year effort to redeem as many of God's creation as possible. I believe the Rapture will occur very soon. Jesus will take His church home, and history will end. This is the plan that Jesus accomplished on the cross.

(This chapter is printed with the gracious permission of Pastor Tony Miano, Evangelist, Grace Fellowship Church, Davenport, IA. While the text of this chapter is mine, the idea of "What did Jesus finish on the cross?" originated with Pastor Miano in an article he wrote some years ago. The article, "Tetelestai, It is finished!" : "Jesus does not need your help" has been republished on Pastor Miano's blog : crossencountersmin. com. I can't thank Tony enough for his gracious permission to use his idea.)

DISCUSSION QUESTIONS

1. Besides the information in this chapter, what else did Jesus finish on the cross?
2. In some circles, it is conventional wisdom that after we die we will have to stand before Jesus and answer for our sins. Do you believe this? Why or why not.
3. Discuss the various theological ideas regarding the Kingdom of God.

Chapter 10

ON SALVATION

"One of the criminals who hung there hurled insults
at him: 'Aren't you the Christ? Save yourself and
us!' But the other criminal rebuked him. 'Don't you
fear God,' he said, 'since you are under the same
sentence? We are punished justly, for we are getting what our deeds deserve. But this man has done
nothing wrong.' Then he said, 'Jesus, remember me
when you come into your kingdom.' Jesus answered
him, 'I tell you the truth, today you will be with me
in paradise'" (Luke 23: 39–43, NIV).

I t was about noon and the ordeal was almost over. Soon Jesus
would cry out with a loud voice, "It is finished" (*Tetelestai*
in Greek), and then give up his spirit (John 19:30). As set out
in the Luke passage above, the last person on Earth that we
know of who Jesus afforded salvation to was the thief, a criminal, hanging on the cross next to him. So, we might ask some
important questions about this most striking event. Who was
this thief? What did he do to gain salvation from Jesus? And
how does this singular event impact our current views in our
own churches about what constitutes true salvation?

First, let's take a look at the Roman Empire itself to see how
those two criminals got up on a Roman cross to begin with.

The Roman Empire was a large and sophisticated commercial enterprise. At its height, Rome controlled trade throughout the Mediterranean, the Ancient Near East, and parts of Europe. The fundamental idea behind Rome's conquests was to secure capital in the form of loot, slaves, food and other goods, as well as wealth of all kinds. This was done through force of arms and the *Pax Romana,* an agreement between Rome and the conquered provinces, which promised peace and protection in exchange for cooperation, particularly in the area of trade. Rome supported itself for hundreds of years from the commerce it derived from other provinces.

So, it is no surprise that Rome wanted nothing more than domestic tranquility to facilitate the uninterrupted flow of commerce. The last thing Rome would tolerate was the disruption of the civil order and particularly any resistance against Rome itself. Acts leading to civil unrest or upsetting the peace and dignity of the Empire got people up on a Roman cross, and I suspect that our two thieves were a great deal more sinister than petty criminals. They may have raided supply trains going to the port in Caesarea, killed a Roman soldier, or committed enough crimes against the local population to cause turmoil. They could also have been Zionist revolutionaries, intent on the overthrow of the Romans. Regardless, the Romans would not have put up with any of this.

In Luke 23: 39-43 the first thief mocked Jesus. He said, "Aren't you the Christ? Save yourself and us!" This is supported by accounts in Mark 15:29–32 and Matthew 27:39–44. The crowd shouted much the same thing to Jesus. That was mob rule at its worst. The short story of Jesus' execution is about the Pharisees, part of the religious and civil government of Palestine, plotting to kill Jesus and then stirring up a mob to cause civil disruption during Passover week. The Sanhedrin, including

Pharisees, Sadducees, and the Chief Priest, was both the religious and civil government of Palestine at the time, and was exclusively controlled by the Jews. The Sanhedrin had a lot of freedom to run things the way they wanted so long as there was domestic tranquility and commercial productivity. The Sanhedrin, however, was limited in what it could do. It could not execute someone of its own accord. It had to appeal to the Roman government if it wanted to have someone executed and gain the Roman government's cooperation to carry out the execution. That was the reason for Jesus' trials before both Jewish and Roman authorities. Everyone had to sign off on it before it could take place.

That is where the mob comes in. The Pharisees incited the citizens and convinced Roman authorities that, even though the Romans did not find Jesus guilty of anything, angry public opinion had them convinced that civil unrest would result if they freed Jesus. I believe that is the dynamic that causes Pontius Pilate to wash his hands of the affair and turn Jesus over to the Jews. Current politicians (Roman officials were definitely politicians), taking a political position to support the loudest and angriest mob voices should surprise no one since it has been going on now for at least two thousand years.

Then there are the thieves themselves. This short passage in Luke tells us a lot about these two men. To begin with, they were Jewish. We know this for certain because of the response of the second thief, when he said, "Don't you fear God?" No pagan, Greek, Roman, or anyone else in the area would have referred to God, particularly in the singular. Further, the use of the phrase "fear God" is a unique Old Testament expression that would not likely be used by anyone except a Jew. And, as we have said, these men were not just petty criminals but more likely very dangerous men.

Finally, we come to the second thief. In the brief words set out in Luke, what did the thief say, and what were the import of those words that he would gain his salvation? First, after rebuking the first thief, the second thief says, "Don't you fear God? ... We are punished justly for we are getting what our deeds deserve." That quote tells us that the thief, being Jewish, was fully aware of God, His requirements, and His Commandments. He also knew that he had not lived as a righteous man but as a wicked one and was going to face judgment before an angry God. Above all, the overriding character of this statement shows that the thief was truly and completely repentant. He didn't want to face God with his sins.

Next, the thief says, "But this man has done nothing wrong." This is an extraordinary statement. I believe the thief knew exactly who Jesus was and was really saying that He was Messiah, the sinless Son of God. Being Jewish, as we think the thief had to be, he may have been exposed to the many Messianic prophecies in the Old Testament. He may have heard Jesus speak and may have even been a follower.

Finally, the thief made his last statement, addressing Jesus himself. He said, "Jesus, remember me when you come into your kingdom." This is a startling statement considering that all three men were within hours—if not minutes—of dying. No one would come down from their crosses alive and the thief knew it. By all estimation, that is a profound statement of faith on the part of the thief. He knew who Jesus was and may have known what would happen in three days. Jesus said he would rise in three days (Mark 14:58 and John 2:19) and maybe the thief had even heard Jesus say it. Even the Apostles may not have fully understood what would happen in three days. Somehow the thief did. He fully understood that Jesus was

Messiah, Lord of Lords, and King of Kings, and would establish the Kingdom of God.

Jesus then gave salvation to the thief with the last words He uttered before He said "It is finished" and died. "I tell you the truth, today you will be with me in paradise." What does that statement tell us about salvation? To begin with, there was no act the thief could do to gain it. There is nothing *we* can do to get salvation, keep it, or perfect it. It is a gift. There is not one thing that man can do to sanctify himself or make himself holy before God. That is why God sent Jesus. Despite man's efforts for thousands of years to work his way up to God, to make himself holy before God, and to work his way into heaven, God had to reach down to man. There is no such thing as works-based Christianity. We can follow all the rules and expectations we want but it won't save us. God had to send Jesus to redeem His creation.

We are all sinful and we all, as Paul said, have fallen short and we always will. But Jesus' message is a simple one. It is a two-step process. All the thief did was repent of his sins and believe that Jesus was Messiah, Son of God, sent to forgive our sins and redeem us to God. That was it. Why do some churches, even now, make salvation more complicated, restrictive, and exclusive with rules and requirements that Jesus never mentioned? There are no rituals, no sacraments, no ceremonies, and nothing we can do or will do to give us salvation. On the cross, Jesus demonstrated the way to salvation.

What happened to the thief after that? Did judgment await him? Was he cast into Hades for his sins? What did Jesus say? Jesus said the thief would be with him in paradise "this day." That meant that same day. Did the thief receive judgment for his sins? Did he face some sort of accounting for them?

It is conventional wisdom in some circles that, when we die, we will appear in heaven and be held to account for all the sins we have committed. Some also believe, from the writing of Paul in 2 Corinthians 5:10 and elsewhere, that there will be a judgment (of sorts) for believers. All due respect, I don't personally believe there is any judgment for Jesus' Church. Nothing in the passage regarding the thief suggests a judgment of any kind. In addition, the thief went directly to "paradise," presumably heaven, with Jesus, and to the home of God. In the sight of God, our sins have already been atoned for by Jesus. Again, there is nothing we can do to attain salvation and heaven that Jesus hasn't already done for us.

Also, this dispels the notions of soul sleep, purgatory, Hades, and any other intermediate steps for believers, on the way to heaven. The transition seems to be immediate.

Additionally, let's look at the Greek word "*Tetelestai*", translated "It is finished". This is the last thing Jesus said on the cross before he died. In the modern era, we have learned that this term was commonly used in the Ancient World as a commercial term. Scholars have found the term stamped on many ancient commercial documents. The term means that the debt is canceled, paid in full, and the debtor is free of any obligation whatsoever, as if the debt had never occurred. When Jesus spoke this one word, I believe everyone, including the thief who repented, who believes in Jesus as Messiah is freed from the bondage and debt of sin, and that sin is cast away, never to be seen again (Ps. 103:11–12).

I think I know what is going to happen when I die. Both the Jews and, later, the Greeks, believed that the soul is immortal. The body is perishable, as we know, but the soul never dies. Our souls consist of everything that is in our head and our heart—the things that make us who we are. Both the Old and

New Testaments support this idea, as well as Jesus himself (Matt. 16:26). Just like the thief, my soul will go to heaven and stand before Jesus. Just like the thief, I'll be there in my scarlet robe of sin with filth all over me. God will say to Jesus, "Son, who is this?" Jesus will respond, "It's OK, Father, he's one of mine." God won't see the pitiful sinner standing there deserving whatever wrath and judgment God would mete out. All God will see is His sinless Son, who always saves his sheep, and who redeemed both the thief and me.

Come to Jesus.

QUESTION

1. Can you clearly and simply explain to the lost the message of salvation?

BIBLIOGRAPHY

CHAPTER 1 -

Allen, Leslie C., *The New International Commentary on the Old Testament, The Books of Joel, Obadiah, Jonah, and Micah* (Grand Rapids: Wm. B. Erdmans Publishing Co., 1976)

Banks, William L., *Jonah the Reluctant Prophet* (Chicago: Moody Press, 1966)

Bauer, Susan Wise, *The History of the Ancient World* (New York: W. W. Norton, 2007)

Chisholm, Robert B. jr., *Handbook on the Prophets* (Grand Rapids: Baker Academic, 2002)

Dever, Mark, *The Message of the Old Testament* (Wheaton: Crossway Books, 2006)

Ellison, H. L., *The Expositors Bible Commentary, Jonah*, Frank E. Gaebelein, Editor (Grand Rapids: Zondervan, 1992)

Hannah, John D., *The Bible Knowledge Commentary*, John F. Walvoord and Roy B. Zuck, Editors (Colorado Springs: David C. Cook, 1984)

Keil, C. F., *Commentary on the Old Testament, The Minor Prophets* (Grand Rapids: William B. Erdmans Publishing Co., 1984)

Glaze, A. J. jr., *The Broadman Bible Commentary, vol. 7, Jonah* (Nashville: Broadman Press, 1970)

Griffiths, Michael C., T*he New International Bible Commentary, Jonah*, F.F. Bruce, General Editor (Grand Rapids: Zondervan Publishing House, 1979)

Phillips, John, *Exploring the Minor Prophets* (Grand Rapids: Kregel Publications, 1998)

Ryrie, Charles Caldwell, The Ryrie Study Bible, Expanded Edition, NIV (Chicago: Moody Press, 1994)

Smith, Billy K. and Frank S. Page, *The New American Commentary, Jonah* (Nashville: B&H Publishing Group, 1995)

CHAPTER 2 -

Dever, Mark, *The Message of the Old Testament* (Wheaton: Crossway Books, 2006)

Gaebelein, Frank E., Editor, *The Expositors Bible Commentary* (Grand Rapids: Zondervan, 1992)

Goldenberg, Robert, "How did Ruth Become the Model Convert", *Conservative Judaism*, 61, no. 3 (Spring, 2010)

Hamilton, Victor P., *Handbook on the Historical Books* (Grand Rapids: Baker Academic, 2001)

Kennedy, J. Hardee, *The Broadman Bible Commentary – Ruth* (Nashville: Broadman Press, 1970)

Linafelt, Tod, "Narrative and Poetic Art in the Book of Ruth", *Journal of Bible and Theology*, 64, no. 2 (April 2010) 117-129

Merrill, Eugene H. , Mark F. Rooker, and Michael A. Grisanti, *The World and the Word* (Nashville: B&H Academic, 2011)

Michael, Matthew, "The Art of Persuasion and the Book of Ruth", *Hebrew Studies: Madison*, 56 (2015)

Reiss, Moshe, "Ruth and Naomi, Foremothers of David", *Jewish Bible Quarterly*, 35, no. 3 (07/2007) 192 et seq.

Ryrie, Charles Caldwell, *The Ryrie Study Bible, Expanded Edition, NIV* (Chicago: Moody Press, 1994)

Strong, James, *The New Strong's Expanded Exhaustive Concordance of the Bible* (Nashville: Thomas Nelson, 2010)

Reed, John W., *The Bible Knowledge Commentary, Walvoord, John F. and Roy B. Zuck, Editors* (Colorado Springs: David C. Cook, 1984)

CHAPTER 3 -

Kaiser, Walter C. and Silva, Moises, *Introduction to Biblical Hermeneutics*, (Grand Rapids: Zondervan, 1994, 2007)

Enns, Paul, *The Moody Handbook of Theology*, (Chicago: Moody Publishers, 1989, 2008, and 2014)

Chafer, Lewis Sperry, *Systematic Theology*, (Dallas Theological Seminary, 1948, 1976)

Pentecost, J. Dwight, *Things to Come*, (Grand Rapids: Zondervan, 1958)

Walton, John H., *Ancient Near East Thought and the Old Testament*, (Grand Rapids: Baker Publishing Group, 2006)

Oswalt, John N., *The Bible Among the Myths*, (Grand Rapids: Zondervan, 2009)

Owens, Mary Frances, *Layman's Bible Book Commentary*, (Nashville: Broadman Press, 1983)

Yamauchi, Edwin, *The Expositors Bible Commentary - Nehemiah*, (Grand Rapids: Zondervan, 1988)

Lockyer, Herbert, *All the Prayers of the Bible*, (Grand Rapids: Zondervan, 1959)

Ryrie, Charles Caldwell, *The Ryrie Study Bible*, (Chicago: Moody Press, 19767, 1978)

Merrill, Eugene H., Mark F. Rooker, and Michael Grisanti, *The World and the Word*, (Nashville: B&H Publishing Group, 2011)

CHAPTER 4 -

Enns, Paul. *The Moody Handbook of Theology*. Chicago: Moody Publishers, 1989, 2008, and 2014

Chafer, Lewis Sperry. *Systematic Theology*. Dallas Theological Seminary, 1948, ,1976

Ryrie, Charles Caldwell. *The Ryrie Study Bible, KJV*. Chicago: Moody Press, 1976, 1978

Ryrie, Charles Caldwell. *The Ryrie Study Bible, Expanded Edition, NIV*. Chicago: Moody Press 1986, 1994

Dean, Kenda Creasy. *Almost Christian*. New York: Oxford University Press,, 2010

Enns, Peter. *The Bible Tells Me So*. New York: HarperCollins, 2014

Smith, Christian and Melinda Denton. T*he National Study of Youth and Religion, 2003, Wave 1*, University of Notre Dame, 2003

Burge, Ryan p. and Paul A. Djupe. *"Truly Inclusive or Uniformly Liberal? An Analysis of the Politics of the Emerging Church."* Journal for the Scientific Study of Religion, 53, no.3, (September 2014) 636-651

McKnight, Scott. *"Five Streams of the Emerging Church"*. Christianity Today. February 2007, 35-39

Tatum, Rich. *"What Willow Creek's Reveal Study Really Tells Us"*. Tatumwebeb.com/blog/2008/06/05

Hunt, Stephen. *"The Emerging Church and its Discontents"*. Journal of Beliefs and Values, 29, no.3 (2008)

Slick, Matt. *"Musings on the Emerging Church"*. Carm.org/musings. 12/16/2007

Noebel, David A. *Understanding the Times*. Eugene: Harvest House Publishers, 1991

Pentecost, J. Dwight. *Things to Come*. Grand Rapids: Zondervan, 1958

Pickowicz, Nate. *"Andy Stanley, Megachurches, and the Bullying of Christ's Bride"*. Christianity (https://entreatingfavor.com/andy-stanley-megachurches-bullying-christ-bride

Chapman, Landon. *"Andy Stanley's Statements about the Bible are not Cutting Edge – They're Old Liberalism*. Christianity (https://entreatingfavor.com/andy-stanley-statements-bible

Kozar, Steve. *"The Andy Stanley Cornucopia of False Teaching, Fast Talking & Postmodern Ambiguity"*. Http://www.piratechristian.com/messedupchurch/2016

Iszler, Madison. *"NC Churches Reach Out to Younger Crowds"*. Jefferson City News Tribune, 11/6/16

Carson, D. A. *Becoming Conversant with the Emerging Church*. Grand Rapids: Zondervan, 2005

Hayek, F. A. *The Fatal Conceit – The Errors of Socialism*. Chicago: The University of Chicago Press, 1988

Sowell, Thomas. *On Classical Economics*. New Haven and London: Yale University Press, 2006

CHAPTER 5 -

Beilby, James K., *Thinking About Christian Apologetics*, Downer's Grove: InterVarsityPress, USA, 2011.

Groothuis, Douglas, *Christian Apologetics: A Comprehensive Case for Biblical Faith*, Downer's Grove: InterVarsityPress, USA, 2011.

Zacharias, Ravi, *Jesus Among Other Gods*, Nashville: Thomas Nelson, 2000

Huntington, Samuel P., *The Clash of Civilizations and The Remaking of World Order*, New York: Simon and Schuster, 1996

Fukuyama, Francis, *The End of History and The Last Man*, New York: Free Press, 1992.

Dean, Kenda Creasy, *Almost Christian*, New York: Oxford University Press, 2010.

Humanist Manifestos, 1 – 1933, II – 1973, and III – Humanism and Its Aspirations – 2003

Enns, Peter, *The Bible Tells Me So*, New York: HarperCollins, 2014

Bauer, Susan Wise, *The History of The Ancient World*, New York: W. W. Norton & Company, 2007.

Bush, L. Rush, *The Advancement*, Nashville: B&H Academic, 2003.

Lewis, C. S., *Mere Christianity*, New York: HarperCollins, 2001.

Hanson, Victor Davis, *Carnage and Culture*, New York: First Anchor Books Edition, 2002.

Grunbaum, Adolph, Chairman, Center for Philosophy of Science, University of Pittsburgh, *The Place of Secular Humanism in*

Current American Political Culture, speech delivered at University of Pittsburgh, May 7, 1987.

Flynn, Tom, *Secular Humanism Defined,* Council for Secular Humanism, http://www.secular humanism.org/index.php/13, accessed 11/22/2017.

A Secular Humanist Declaration, Council for Democratic and Secular Humanism, http://www.secularhumanism.org/index.php/11, accessed 11/22./2017.

Kurtz, Paul, *Neo-Humanist Statement of Secular Principles and Values: Personal, Progressive, and Planetary,* The Institute for Science and Human Values, http://instituteforscienceandhumanvalues.com/articles/neo-humanist-statement, accessed 11/23/2017.

Chapter 6 -

Betenson, Toby, "Anti-Theodicy", *Philosophy Compass,* 11, no.1, 24 January, 2016.

Boyd, Gregory A., *Satan and the Problem of Evil,* Madison: InterVarsity Press, 2001.

Chafer, Lewis Sperry, *Systematic Theology,* Grand Rapids: Kregel Publications, 1976.

Culp, John, "Overcoming the Limits of Theodicy", *Springer,* 21 May 2015.

Dunnington, Kent, "The Problem With the Satan Hypothesis", *Sophia,* 57, no.2, June, 2018.

Elwell, Walter A., Editor, *Evangelical Dictionary of Theology, Second Edition,* Grand Rapids: Baker Academic, 2001.

Enns, Paul, *The Moody Handbook of Theology,* Chicago: Moody Publishers, 2014.

Erickson, Millard J., *Christian Theology, Third Edition,* Grand Rapids: Baker Academic, 2013.

Geisler, Norman L., *If God, Why Evil?,* Grand Rapids: Baker Publishing Group, 2011.

Groothuis, Douglas, *Christian Apologetics*, Downers Grove: InterVarsity Press, 2011.

Lewis, C. S., *Mere Christianity*, New York: HarperCollins Publishers, 2001.

Moser, Paul K., Theodicy, Christology, and "Divine Hiding: Neutralizing the Problem of Evil," *The Expository Times*, 9 November, 2017.

Trakakis, Nick, "Theodicy: The Solution to the Problem of Evil, or Part of the Problem?", *Sophia*, 47, no. 2, 29 July, 2008.

Vroman, Brian, "The Problem of Evil and the Poverty of the Free Will Theodicy", *Think, Cambridge*, 8, no.22, Summer, 2009.

CHAPTER 7 -

Benware, Paul N., *Understanding End Times Prophecy*, Chicago: Moody Publishers, 2006.

Chafer, Lewis Sperry, *Systematic Theology*, Grand Rapids: Kregel Publications, 1976)

Cloe-Turner, Ronald "The Singularity of the Rapture: Transhumanist and Popular Christian Views of the Future", *Zygon* 47, no. 4 (December 2012) 777-790.

Enns, Paul, *The Moody Handbook of Theology*, Chicago: Moody Publishers, 2014.

Ice, Thomas D. "Why the Doctrine of the Pretribulational Rapture Did Not Begin with Margaret Macdonald." *Bibliotheca Sacra* 147:586 (April 1990) 155-172.

Gribben, Crawford "Rapture Fictions and the Changing Evangelical Condition." *Literature & Theology* 18, no. 1, (March 2004) 77-94.

LaHaye, Time, *Revelation Unveiled*, Grand Rapids: Zondervan, 1999.

Lindsey, Hal, *There's a New World Coming*, Eugene: Harvest House, 1984.

Lindsey, Hal, *Vanished*, Beverly Hills: Western Front Limited, 1999.

Osborne, Grant R., *Revelation*, Grand Rapids: Baker Academic, 2002.

Pentecost, J. Dwight, *Things to Come*, Grand Rapids: Zondervan, 1958.

Ryrie, Charles C., *What You Should Know About the Rapture*, Chicago: Moody Press, 1981.

Stendal, Russell M., *Revelation Unveiled*, Abbotsford: Aneko Press, 2015.

Strong, James, *The New Strong's Expanded Exhaustive Concordance of the Bible*, Nashville: Thomas Nelson, 2010.

Svigel, Michael J. "The Apocalypse of John and the Rapture of the Church: A Reevaluation." *Trinity Journal* 22, no. 1 (Spring 2001) 23-59.

Sweetnam, Mark S. "Hal Lindsay and the Great Dispensational Mutation." *Journal of Religion and Popular Culture* 23, no. 2, (July 2011) 217-235.

Trelstad, Merit, "Death and Apocalypse in a Time of Fear." *Dialog* 57, no. 4 (December 2018) 18 pages.

Walliss, John, "Celling the End Times: The Contours of Contemporary Rapture Films." *Journal of Religion and Popular Culture* 19 (Summer 2008) 1-15.

Walvoord, John F., *The Rapture Question*, Grand Rapids: Zondervan, 1979.

Walvoord, John F., *Revelation*, Chicago: Moody Publishers, 2011.

CHAPTER 8 –

Enns, Paul, The Moody Handbook of Theology, Chicago: Moody Publishers, 1989, 2008, 2014

Ryrie, Charles Caldwell, The Ryrie Study Bible, Expanded Edition, NIV, Chicago: Moody Press, 1986, 1994

Lea, Thomas D. , and David Alan Black, The New Testament: Its Background and Message, Second Edition, Nashville: B&H Publishing Group, 2003

Pentecost, J. Dwight, Things to Come, Grand Rapids: Zondervan, 1958

Kaiser, Walter C. Jr. and Moises Silva, Introduction to Biblical Hermeneutics, Grand Rapids: Zondervan, 1994, 2007

LaHaye, Tim, and Thomas Ice, Charting the End Times, Eugene: Harvest Home Publishers, 2001

Noll, Mark A., Turning Points, 3rd Edition, Grand Rapids: Baker Academic, 1997, 2000, 2012

Kostenberger, Andreas, L. Scott Kellum, and Charles L. Quarles, The Cradle, The Cross, and The Crown: An Introduction to The New Testament, Second Edition, Nashville: B&H Academic, 2009, 2016

CHAPTER 9 -

Ryrie, Charles Caldwell, The Ryrie Study Bible, Expanded Edition, NIV, (Chicago: Moody Press, 1994)

CHAPTER 10 -

Bauer, Susan Wise, The History of the Ancient World, (New York: w. w. Norton, 2007)

Ryrie, Charles Caldwell, The Ryrie Study Bible, Expanded Edition, NIV, (Chicago: Moody Press, 1994)

CPSIA information can be obtained
at www.ICGtesting.com
Printed in the USA
LVHW101525200223
739934LV00005B/613